W9-CRL-064

how
PROGRESSIVES
Rewrote
the
CONSTITUTION

how
PROGRESSIVES
Rewrote
the
CONSTITUTION

RICHARD A. EPSTEIN

CATO
INSTITUTE
WASHINGTON, D.C.

Library of Congress Cataloging-in-Publication Data

Epstein, Richard A., 1943-
   How progressives rewrote the Constitution / Richard A. Epstein.
     p. cm.
   Includes bibliographical references.
   ISBN 1-930865-87-2 (cloth : alk. paper) 1. Constitutional history—
United States. 2. Progressivism (United States politics) I. Title.

KF4541.E67 2006
342.7302'9—dc22   2005044891

Cover design by Jon Meyers.
Printed in the United States of America.

CATO INSTITUTE
1000 Massachusetts Ave., N.W.
Washington, D.C. 20001
www.cato.org

⬲ Contents ⬳

≈ Preface ≈

Why We Must Reopen Closed Debates

On September 17, 2004, I delivered the Cato Institute's third annual B. Kenneth Simon Lecture in Constitutional Thought.* The topic on which I chose to speak was the intellectual development of the Progressive movement of which I had long been critical on constitutional, economic, and philosophical grounds. More specifically, I offered a full defense of the earlier constitutional protection of economic

*This volume is an extended version of that lecture. My thanks to Roger Pilon for inviting me to give the lecture, for organizing the event and pushing me hard to write it up in complete form, and for his editorial assistance; and to Rachel Kovner of the Stanford Law School, class of 2006, whose unerring and critical eye much improved this manuscript. Her tireless labor on short deadlines has gone far beyond the standard duties of a research assistant. My thanks also to Dennis Hutchinson and Geoffrey R. Stone for reading through an earlier draft of the manuscript and offering many suggestions for its improvement. The errors that remain are mine alone.

liberties—the right to dispose of one's labor and property as one sees fit, and a limited view of federal power under the Commerce Clause of the United States Constitution. To many, lawyers and laymen alike, there seems to be little reason to unearth a set of legal controversies that had sorted themselves out by the middle of the New Deal in favor of expanded government power. If the Progressives remade the Constitution in their own image, so what? History is history, and politics is politics, and never the twain shall meet. Don't reopen old debates and painful wounds.

That attitude may be appropriate for many fields, but it does not sit quite right with legal disputes. Here, precedent always plays its part, because it is sometimes thought that the respect for the accumulated wisdom of the past counts as one protection against the use of arbitrary power in the future. But I suspect that the reasons for not revisiting these constitutional issues go deeper. Although science is capable of linear advancement, the same is not true of law, where the same insights and mistakes tend to recur again and again. My first course of legal study was Roman law (as an ersatz Englishman at Oxford in 1964), which I still teach on a regular basis. The private law controversies that generate such animated discussions among lawyers and scholars today were often argued with great ingenuity and imagination hundreds of years ago. The traditional classical liberal ideas of constitutional government—private property and freedom of contract, coupled with limited government and low levels of taxation and regulation, and, in the American context, federalism—may be traced to ancient times. They had a profound influence during the fertile founding period of our own Constitution. As historical landmarks, they stand as a constant reminder that it is possible to think of constitutional law without embracing the ideals of the modern social welfare state.

These debates swirl around many modern controversies, but they often come to a head whenever a new Supreme Court nomination is in the wings. However great my affection for the classical ideals that animated some, but not all, of the pre–New Deal jurisprudence, the opposition to that position is every bit as intense. Proponents of the modern position often make their lives far easier than they ought to be by their own extravagant misdescriptions of key doctrines of the now-reviled "Old Court." They are quite happy to place anyone opposed to their ideals in an imaginary "Constitution-in-Exile" movement, as though employing that term (Judge Douglas Ginsburg coined it) makes their opponents as legitimate as, say, deposed Bourbon royalists yearning for a return to some bygone age.

Overblown rhetoric to one side, just what might such a supposed movement support? We are often told that defenders of the pre–New Deal world order believe in an "unregulated America," when what they typically support is a legal order that does not regulate the prices, terms, and conditions on which goods and services are sold in a competitive market. It is often said that defenders of the pre–New Deal world believe that all property rights are inviolable. In fact, the classical liberal tradition in which I write accepts proportionate taxation. It also insists that government at all levels can use the power of eminent domain but only for public uses and upon payment of just compensation. That position also accepts the use of a police power that allows for regulation without compensation, which historically embraced law that addressed the public health, safety, morals, and general welfare, to use the formulation followed in the controversial case of *Lochner v. New York*.[1] In some cases, that theory (like much of the modern law of privacy and sexual association) rejects some pre–New Deal legislation, such as that which is intended to promote the "morals" of the public at large. The classical liberal position is not "frozen" in the past; nor does it line up with modern left/right or Red/Blue divisions. The constant theme that drives the analysis is that of small government, which offers as little comfort to the new generation of religious and social conservatives as it does to the traditional American left.

Of course, I endorse some propositions that many other critics of modern American constitutional law most emphatically do not accept. Years ago, in my 1985 book *Takings*, I took the position that the standard interferences with employment contracts, such as minimum wage laws, antidiscrimination laws (in competitive markets only), collective bargaining laws, and Social Security requirements, were unconstitutional, all on the ground that the state has no better knowledge of what individuals need than individuals themselves do.[2] I stand unapologetically by those positions today and think that the invalidation of those programs rests not on some narrowly egoistical view of private property but on the correct *social* ground that this view does us more good in the long run than the endless creation of various "unfair" practices, such as those under modern labor law, that introduce various forms of state monopolies, each of which further saps the productive juices from American society. At the same time, I fully recognize that the mistakes of the past, such as the creation of Social Security, cannot be undone today in light of the extensive reliance interests that have been created. Many institutions that are not defensible as a matter of first principle become so embedded in our social life that they cannot be undone without grievous harm. But that acceptance of change should never be confused with the mistaken belief that long usage of accepted doctrine renders it necessarily immune from rational criticism and constitutional change; for if that were the case, then the doctrine of "separate-but-equal," announced in 1896 in *Plessy v. Ferguson*,[3] would have been affirmed, not overturned 58 years later in *Brown v. Board of Education*.[4] There is no easy metric to solve the "second-best" of what, if anything, should be done to correct past constitutional errors.

Critics of the classical liberal position have a field day in thinking that positions such as my own (and others still more modest in their intentions) will "turn the clock back" and so plunge us into some legal Dark Age. Thinking of this sort played a minor role in the confirmation hearings of John G. Roberts Jr. to replace the late Chief Justice William H. Rehnquist. Roberts was, of course, confirmed by a comfortable 78-22 margin. But the hearings were replete with rumblings in high places—including by no less a figure than the Republican Chairman of the Committee, Arlen Specter—that revealed an unsympathetic attitude toward the modest incursions on the New Deal Commerce Clause jurisprudence. The sentence that gives rise to the offense will strike anyone who is not steeped in the Court's convoluted Commerce Clause jurisprudence as odd. In his dissent from a denial of en banc review in *Rancho Viejo, LLC v. Norton* Roberts questioned whether using the Endangered Species Act to protect "a hapless toad that, for reasons of its own, lives its entire life in California constitutes regulating 'Commerce . . . among the several States.'"[5]

These constant discussions in Senate confirmation hearings of our constitutional past make clear that the political arena is not closed to further public deliberations about the proper understanding of our constitutional system, and of the role of the United States Supreme Court within that system. Critics of the classical liberal position happily brand as "radicals" or "extreme right-wing ideologues" anyone who holds views that remotely resemble my own. Their goal is to exclude those views in selecting Supreme Court justices and in framing the constitutional agenda of the next generation. I have written this book in part to correct what I believe to be pervasive misconceptions about the central features of the pre–New Deal constitutional legal order—chiefly, federalism and economic liberties—features that in certain key aspects should be preferred to our current constitutional legal structures. Even more, I hope that this critique of the conventional wisdom on these vital issues will help inform readers of the ability of these now discarded views to lead us toward sound constitutional government in the years to come.

Richard A. Epstein
Chicago, Illinois
October 10, 2005

⇜ 1 ⇝

Introduction

American constitutional law has not followed a single unbroken path from the founding period to the present day. In many ways the key turning point for both federalism and individual rights came with the Supreme Court's final vindication of Franklin Roosevelt's New Deal legislation in the Court's decisive 1936 term. It was then that the Court bowed to the New Deal, shortly after Roosevelt unveiled his infamous Court-packing scheme—his threat to pack a recalcitrant Court with six new members.[6] Widely touted as "the switch in time that saved nine,"[7] the key elements of that switch are aligned along two dimensions. The first concerns structural issues relating to our federal system. The second concerns the extent to which the various substantive protections of liberty and property found in the original Constitution and the amendments thereto limited the ability of government, federal and state, to regulate the economic system.

It is important, however, not to compress the entire shift into one critical term. Since 1900 there had been many conflicts over various government schemes, and government power over such key matters as taxation, rent control, zoning, lending, and rate regulation had expanded in the pre-1937 period. But the 1936 term was distinctive in that it put to rest all the ongoing debates over federalism and individual rights that had raged in earlier years. The New Deal Court thus vindicated both expansive federal powers and limited protection of individual rights of liberty and property against both federal and state regulation. That transformation represents the defining moment in modern American constitutional law: the Court's shift toward the big government model that continues to dominate today.

The tumultuous events of the New Deal Era did not take place in a vacuum, however. They grew out of the intellectual work of the Progressive Era, which inaugurated the fundamental shift in American constitutional thought. The Progressives were the self-conscious social and legal reformers who occupied center stage in the period roughly from the onset of the 20th century through the election of Franklin Delano Roosevelt as president in 1932. They exerted a considerable influence on legal and constitutional theory in the years before Roosevelt took over the presidency. In addition, most of the innovative, if controversial, domestic programs of the New Deal were in fact direct outgrowths of the Progressive campaign for larger, more active government during the 30-plus years preceding the watershed events of 1937.

To understand the importance of the Progressive movement to modern constitutional theory and politics, one might find useful a summary of its key social and legal positions, most of which were articulated in opposition to the dominant social and legal thought of the Old Court—"old" as in antiquated or outdated—whose principles it successfully displaced. First, as a general matter, Progressives believed in the power of science and economics, employed by government, to lift up the economic and social position of the general population. In this regard, they were influenced in part by Bismarckian social initiatives in 19th-century Germany, which had pioneered various forms of worker protection and social insurance. Second, to achieve their expansive social ends, Progressives adopted a "realist" jurisprudence that broke sharply from the then-dominant "formalist" approach to law, which they dismissed as "blind" to the massive power shifts in social relations that took place with industrialization following the Civil War.

The theme was put forcefully by the young Roscoe Pound in his well-known essays, "Mechanical Jurisprudence"[8] (an approach he did not like) and "The Need of a Sociological Jurisprudence"[9] (which he took as self-evident). For Progressives, the new change in circumstances was enough to dismiss unhesitatingly

Adam Smith's happy conception of the "invisible hand," which envisioned the close alignment of private and social interests in ordinary market transactions. Now that bargains did not result from equals haggling by the back fence over the price of a cow, new and strenuous state action was needed to offset the dominance of large firms over both customers and employees. Writing in 1917 about those developments and the need for modern "living" law, Louis Brandeis expressed the new view well when he castigated traditional formalist judges for their blind adherence—in the face of new realities—to outmoded 18th-century conceptions of liberty:

> Yet, while invention and discovery created the possibility of releasing men and women from the thraldom of drudgery, there actually came, with the introduction of the factory system and the development of the business corporation, new dangers to liberty. Large publicly owned corporations replaced small privately owned concerns. Ownership of the instruments of production passed from the workman to the employer. Individual personal relations between the proprietor and his help ceased. The individual contract of service lost its character, because of the inequality in position between employer and employee. The group relation of employee to employer with collective bargaining became common; for it was essential to the workers' protection.

Legal Science Static. Political as well as economic and social science noted these revolutionary changes. But legal science—the unwritten or judge-made laws as distinguished from legislation—was largely deaf and blind

4

to them. Courts continued to ignore newly arisen social needs. They applied complacently 18th century conceptions of the liberty of the individual and of the sacredness of private property. Early 19th century scientific half-truths like "The survival of the fittest," which translated into practice meant "The devil take the hindmost," were erected by judicial sanction into a moral law.[10]

In writing those prophetic passages, Brandeis offered no empirical evidence about the deleterious effects of the inequality of bargaining power on the operation of the economic system, which includes an indictment of the Old Court attitude toward child labor, women in the workforce, and overall wage levels. But some rudimentary numbers, readily available today, tell a rather different story. Here is one set of figures, among many that could be gathered, that speaks to the claim that inequality of bargaining power should be regarded as all-pervasive in the labor market.

	Total Workers (thousands)	Workers, Ages 10 to 15 (thousands)	(%)	Female Workers (thousands)	(%)
1900	29,073	1,750	6.02	5,319	18.3
1910	37,371	1,622	4.34	7,445	19.92
1920	42,434	1,417	3.34	8,637	20.35
1930	48,830	667	1.37	10,752	22.02[11]

It takes little ingenuity to see that child labor was already on the wane by 1918, the time that the Supreme

Court explicitly held that Congress could not regulate the matter.[12] During this same period, it is worth noting that for "lower skilled labor" the hour figures showed a similar reduction. The average number of hours worked per week in manufacturing industries shrank continuously from 59 in 1900 to just over 50 in 1926, while average wages per hour for those industries moved up from just over $0.21 to just over $0.64, a more than threefold increase. Notwithstanding shorter hours, the pay packet swelled from $12.39 to $32.00, a 2.58-fold increase when the value of the dollar did not quite double.[13] And life expectancy stood at around 47 years in 1900; by 1910 that figure moved up to 50 years; by 1920 it was up to 54 years; and by 1930 it was close to 60 years, with women retaining a statistical edge over men throughout.[14] Just to keep matters in perspective—the rate of increase slowed down during the Depression but then picked up again, so that by 1950, life expectancy reached over 68 years, up from just under 63 years in 1940.[15]

These statistics are not meant to be selective. Anyone can go back to the *Historical Statistics* to find more detailed gradations that reveal the same basic point. A steady state of material progress persisted until the Depression, and did so while the "outdated" constitutional doctrines of the Old Court largely continued to hold sway. The exact source of these improvements is hard to pin down. Without question, many of them are attributable to public health measures dealing with such matters as sewage and sanitation. Yet that does nothing to discredit the justices of the Old Court, who had given their ready assent to these measures.[16] Public health improvements, while critical to increased life expectancy, do not explain the increase in wages, the decrease in hours worked, and the declining importance of child labor in that period. On those employment issues, the justices of the Old Court often resisted the move toward regulation.

If the Old Court's constitutional approach was so destructive, however, we should not have seen improvements across the board. The obvious explanation for those improvements is that increases in technology and productivity redounded to the benefit of all, just as the "obsolete" analysis of Adam Smith had predicted. Yet the faux empiricism of the Progressives did not acknowledge any ground-level progress that might undercut their own powerful rhetorical edge. Start from their tendentious view of American history, and the implications for political and legal action become clear. The Progressive view of social progress equated active government with good government. Predictably, their theory of good government generated a compatible constitutional theory. Thus, any constitutional doctrine that stood in the way of comprehensive reforms had to be rejected or circumvented.

The Progressive program was deeply dismissive of the "individualist" ethic that Progressives believed shaped traditional social attitudes toward the transformation of social life. In consequence, they thought that it was necessary to undermine in two distinct areas traditional legal conceptions rooted in that bygone ethic. The first of these concerned the structure of American federalism, in which a national government of enumerated powers had a few defined tasks, with all else, including the regulation of economic activity, left largely to the states. The second had to do with the protection of individual liberty that dominated the judicial thinking of the time—chiefly the liberty of entering into voluntary contracts with whomever one pleased, and only with such people.

On the first point, Progressives were champions of economic nationalism with its cardinal principle that the extensive interconnection of all aspects of the American economy cried out for federal regulation. They held that Congress could enact that legislation pursuant to its power to regulate commerce among the several states under Article I, section 8, clause 3 of the Constitution. On the second point, they thought that ever greater inequalities of wealth justified overriding constitutionally protected rights of liberty, property, and contract. In all of this, the "public interest" was to rank supreme. In one sense, the argument was that the interests of some privileged class always came out second in the social calculus. In another sense, the approach appeared even more strident: the public interest was defined in opposition to, rather than as inclusive of, the welfare of the rich and powerful in the social order. So powerful was this urge to regulate ordinary business that Progressives often extended their regulatory impulse uncritically to personal liberties, including reproductive and religious rights, lest protecting those would undermine their program for economic reform.

The struggle between Progressives and traditionalists took place on both a functional and a textual level. Before that struggle can be examined in any depth, however, it is necessary to deal with a few preliminaries on constitutional theory. The first point has to do with the uses and limits of constitutional textualism. Any sensible theory of constitutional law must take the key terms in a document and give them the meaning that ordinary users would have attached to them when the provisions were drafted. It is usually dangerous business to put a modern gloss on a traditional term.

By the same token, however, it must be understood that this textual enterprise is only the first stage of the larger business of constitutional interpretation. Many of the key questions of constitutional law have to do with the articulation of doctrines that have no particular textual origin, but whose inclusion is fairly required by the text itself. As becomes clear later, the proper rendering of the police power—the ability of the state to act to advance health, safety, morals, or the general welfare—is one of the critical elements of constitutional law.[7] Yet the term "police power" itself (or any of its variants) appears nowhere in the text of the Constitution. Still, so long as the articulation of legal rules is regarded as a process of successive qualifications of some basic principle—as has long been the case—then this task is part of the constitutional inquiry.

This approach to constitutional interpretation will not seem strange to those versed in the private law, which employs the same process in dealing with private disputes between ordinary individuals. That entire body of law is organized around the view that the plaintiff gives a prima facie account of the defendant's wrong, for which some justification or excuse is offered by the defendant. With public bodies, the notion of *excuse*—"yes, it was wrong, but I could not help myself because I was young, sick, feeble, or insane"—does not resonate, for public actors are rightly presumed to be capable of discharging their functions. But by the same token, the idea of public *justification*—"yes, we did infringe your rights, but for good reason, and we would do it again if the situation called for it"—is very much part of the constitutional discourse. Hence, the accurate explication of the constitutional text requires here—as in so many other situations—the necessary implication of a nontextual source of constitutional law, which can only be understood in light of the function, purposes, and objectives of the original document, coupled with its subsequent amendments, many of which alter that original balance in important ways.

Once the nontextual elements are given their due, then any adequate theory of constitutional law must address the level of scrutiny the Court should apply in exercising its power of judicial review—that is, its power to strike down statutes because they are in conflict with provisions of the Constitution. Clearly, this matter is of immense importance, because the harder a court looks at any given piece of legislation, the more likely it will find that the law violates some structural or substantive provision of the Constitution. Concern with levels of judicial scrutiny received its formal elaboration only after the Progressive Era, but the modern terminology often helps with understanding the actions in question.

At one pole, the Court could take a position of high deference to congressional action, which it does when it invokes the somewhat misnamed "rational basis" test. The test takes its name from Justice Holmes's famous dissent in *Lochner v. New York*,[18] which indicated that courts should bend over backward not to upset the considered judgment of the legislature. At the opposite extreme is the standard of "strict scrutiny," which says that a statute that touches on a protected constitutional right is necessarily unconstitutional unless the end it serves rises to the level of a "compelling state interest" and the means chosen are "narrowly tailored" to achieve that well-defined objective. In the middle, but closer in practice to the strict scrutiny standard, lies "intermediate scrutiny," which requires the Court to strike down any statute that does not bear a reasonable means-ends relationship to a "legitimate state interest." The conflict between the Old Court and the Progressives was not over whether strict or intermediate scrutiny was more appropriate to the cases on which they disagreed. Rather, the Progressives' claim, cast in modern terms, was that a rational-basis approach should apply to all conflicts between government power and individual rights to property and contract, while the Old Court defended some higher standard of judicial review.

To see how all of this plays out, it is useful to give a more complete account of the legal regime the Progressives sought to displace. We begin, therefore, with a brief look at what a classical liberal regime requires before turning to the question of whether and to what extent the Constitution embodies such a regime. Once that basic outline is established, we can then turn to the doctrinal issues at stake, beginning with federalism and then turning to individual rights. In neither case do we see in the traditional view of the Old Court anything like a dogmatic or reflexive protection of either state interests or individual rights. The full picture of the traditional view is far more complex than the Progressive caricature of it and, accordingly, requires some careful explication. Once the older positions are stated with some accuracy, it is possible to return to those same topics, federalism and individual rights, to see how Progressive innovations changed the landscape. This will show the major transformation Progressivism wrought and provide a deeper picture of historical and intellectual crosscurrents. In so doing, I hope to show how the differences in world view influenced judicial behavior on both the federalism and the individual rights issues that confronted the Court up to and through the great constitutional transformation that culminated in the spring of 1937. Here, as everywhere else, ideas have social consequences.

In addition, it is imperative to bring this debate forward into modern times, for the Progressive influence continues to exert itself long past the New Deal, in modern Supreme Court decisions that address questions of federalism,[19] economic liberties,[20] and takings for public use.[21] It seems fair to say that the widely discredited classical liberal synthesis of both federal power and individual rights looks far more attractive to the common man, especially given the Court's total unwillingness to breathe any limits into the requirement that property, even with just compensation, be taken only for "public use." Attitudes toward government continue to shift, and no longer do most people have unquestioned faith in the desire or ability of the government to act only in the public interest. Given this modern unease, the contrast between the classical liberal era and the Progressive Era is a topic of both historical and current interest.

⮞ 2 ⮜

The Classical Liberal Synthesis

A. First Principles

My purpose here is not to defend in full the classical liberal position, because I have undertaken that task on numerous other occasions.[22] But we do need to note the essentials of that position and explain how it differs from the pure libertarian theory with which it is closely allied. As with libertarian theory, the classical liberal position begins with a deep respect for individual choice on the ground that individuals have the best (not perfect, but best) knowledge of their own preferences and desires. Moreover, their actions are presumed to be proper because they advance the interest of at least one person and thus create, other things being equal, some form of social improvement. But that presumption, while a thumb on the social scale, is not absolute, given the effects, both positive and negative, that all human actions have on other people.

At this point, the classical liberal, like the libertarian, seeks to identify those actions whose adverse effects are so great that some steps should be taken to curtail them to enhance, as the phrase goes, the "like liberty" of others. The key acts that fall into this prohibited category are the use of force and fraud. Apart from the simple claim to be left alone, the main behavior that is protected against those twin offenses is the freedom to engage in market competition—to make offers to do business with others. The private voluntary contracts that may result are positive-sum games for the parties to them, and whatever harm ordinary contracts of sale and hire wreak upon competitors (and it is a real harm, no doubt) is more than offset by the gains to the parties and to consumers. We are all systematically better off, therefore, in a regime in which all can enter and exit markets at will than in a social situation in which one person, armed with the monopoly power of government, can license or proscribe the actions of others.

To maintain this view, however, it is essential to resist the perennial pressure by aggrieved individuals to equate market forces with economic duress and then equate economic duress with the use or threat of force. That system of false analogies does not work. The key insight is this: competition is a positive-sum game, while aggression is a negative-sum game. For that social reason, and not for any fascination with the "possessive individualism" that the Progressives denounced, the former should be favored and protected while the latter is deplored and restricted. Individual control over one's labor and property should be governed, therefore, by the principle that competition and aggression are polar opposites. Competition enhances social welfare. Aggression diminishes it.

This emphasis on freedom of choice and freedom of contract shows the close parallels between libertarian and classical liberal thought. But one must also attend to the differences, while noting that the Constitution is unambiguously in the classical liberal camp. The pure libertarian finds it difficult, perhaps impossible, to accept any forced exchanges initiated by the state for the common good. Hence, all forms of taxation and condemnation are categorically ruled out of bounds.[23] At this point, the classical liberal departs from the pure libertarian on the ground that some form of state power is needed to preserve the liberties that both groups believe should be protected. Our Constitution is a classical liberal document insofar as it recognizes, implicitly, an inherent state police power that allows collective action to enforce the criminal laws against force and fraud, to prevent nuisances, and otherwise to restrain activities that violate the rights of others. In addition, the classical liberal position holds that those dangerous activities cannot be countered in practice solely by self-help and other forms of coordinated voluntary action and thus secures

16

an explicit and necessary, if uneasy, place for both taxation and eminent domain.

Indeed, the classical liberal position goes further in two key respects.[24] First, it argues that one function of tax revenues is to pay for infrastructure in the form of highways and public utilities, although these are often privately owned but subject to rate regulation. With respect to such private entities, the classical liberal position looks to limit the economic power of businesses that hold monopoly positions without confiscating their invested capital. Second, the classical liberal position accepts the proposition that certain forms of market failure require, or at least allow, some form of government intervention. Thus, government may restrict the acquisition, under the rule of first possession, of forms of wildlife and natural resources that are subject to premature dissipation through the standard common-pool problem: the party who takes fish or wildlife gets all the gain, but suffers only a tiny fraction of the long-term losses. State regulation of some form is needed to counter the potential for overconsumption.[25] Moreover, and of greater importance here, government may constrain the operation of a private monopoly in favor of competition under some form of antitrust laws.

All of those additional powers are subject, of course, to the general restriction that the means in question must be well adapted to the end. It will not do to allow the state, whose activities are always looked at with suspicion, to declare simply that its activity serves some legitimate government function. Chief Justice Marshall was right to say that the power to tax is the power to destroy.[26] With sufficient foresight, he might well have added that the power to *designate* is the power to destroy. No private business could survive if the state could simply announce that the business has been branded a nuisance or a monopoly without the state's having first to make its case. The issue is as much one of procedural due process, and the right to be heard, as it is of substantive rights. Nor is this level of protection a threat to the public at large. On one hand, as acknowledged by every member of the Old Court, we most certainly need a police power, but one that serves only to protect the health and safety of the public at large.[27] On the other hand, state statutes that suppress market competition in the name of protecting health and safety should be rejected. Private monopolies and cartels, with their control over price and output, can deviate from the ideal conditions of competition. But state-created monopolies and cartels are *worse* because they are not subject to erosion by new entry by outsiders and cheating by cartel members.

Thus, the classical liberal allows greater scope for government action than the hard-line libertarian. As a result, the classical liberal escapes the vulnerabilities of the libertarian line by accepting that private action (excluding only force or fraud) may lead to destructive results. But that said, the classical liberal joins the libertarian in a full-throated condemnation of state power used to create or perpetuate economic monopolies and private cartels in what would otherwise be competitive industries.

The touchstone of the analysis that follows, therefore, is this: state power that may be used to limit monopoly power should never be converted into a force that creates or perpetuates monopoly power. The watchwords are limited government, private property, and freedom of conduct. How, then, does the American constitutional experience stack up against that ideal? Let us first look at the Old Court and then at the Progressives themselves. To facilitate the inquiry, it is useful to divide matters into two parts. The first deals with the structural issues of federalism; the second with individual rights, chiefly but not exclusively in the economic arena.

B. The Old Court Federalism

A little probing shows how those questions of political theory shape our understanding of the American system of federalism. Federalism allows for federal regulation of private business activities at two levels: transactions among states and those between the national government and the states. Yet the connection between federalism and the underlying theory of individual rights is obscured to some extent by the unavoidable trick that the American constitutional experience played on the admittedly different social contract theories of Hobbes and Locke. Both philosophers stressed that the social contract involved ordinary individuals, ostensibly in some state of nature, surrendering some fraction of their liberty and property to the state to obtain in exchange the greater security for their remaining assets that a system of state order promised. In line with that general theory, the prime functions of the state were to restrain violence, to provide for needed social infrastructure, and to ensure the reliable and impartial resolution of individual disputes by neutral judges and other public officials.

However powerful those influences were on key members of the founding generation, they were expressed more clearly in the state constitutions than in the federal Constitution. The national government was not straightforwardly a contract among individuals, even if the opening words of the preamble read, "We the People." More precisely, the Constitution did not seek to take individuals out of a state of nature and put them into civil society. Negotiated by individuals who were all members of state delegations, the Constitution in many key points addressed the distribution of governmental powers over the activities of individuals between the states and the federal government. The rights of individual citizens against their own state governments were much more the province of the state constitutions, most of which contained references to the preservation of liberty and property as the proper ends of government.[28] It is largely for this reason that the *Federalist Papers* (published before the adoption of the Bill of Rights) contain so few references to the then-dominant natural law philosophy, which applied largely to the relationship between the individual and the state. It is not as though the Framers were indifferent to such ideas. It is that they had a different task, in which the protection of individual rights was not foremost on their mind—at least until it became necessary to add a bill of rights to secure state ratification.

On the structural issues of paramount importance to the new Constitution, there was of course no single theory of how powers should be apportioned among the various parts of government. Nor were there clear precedents on how this division should be achieved. The basic deal struck in Philadelphia recognized the importance of national control over copyrights and patents;[29] it contemplated a uniform system of bankruptcy and immigration;[30] it authorized the United States to coin money and to set uniform standards of weights and measures;[31] it gave Congress the power to establish post roads;[32] it created a coordinated scheme of divided power for the training and control of the state militias;[33] and, most relevant for our purposes, it gave Congress "the power . . . to regulate Commerce with foreign Nations, and among the several States, and with the Indian tribes."[34] In addition, the Constitution limited the power of states to act in certain ways. Thus, the states could not pass bills of attainder, ex post facto laws, or laws impairing the obligation of contracts.[35] The states had only a limited power, without the consent of Congress, to impose import duties or taxes insofar as they were "absolutely necessary" to enforce inspection laws.[36]

One obvious question concerns the extent to which that division of power was intended to create a system of government that worked in accordance with classical liberal principles, most concretely by creating a nation that was dedicated to the principles of free trade that so animated Adam Smith's *Wealth of Nations*. The answer to that question is, as with all great constitutional questions, decidedly mixed. The restrictions on import duties and taxation and on the impairment of contracts—together with the implicit restriction on the state regulation of interstate commerce found in the Commerce Clause—were directed to ensure that *states* did not compromise the operation of trade and commerce in a national market. But there was no parallel restriction on the power of *Congress* to restrain trade in its exercise of the commerce power at the national level. Thus, *The Federalist No. 11* observes that the power of Congress to regulate foreign commerce was included with an eye to adopting a national approach that allows the United States to close off its ports to foreign nations: "By prohibitory regulations, extending, at the same time, throughout the States, we may oblige foreign countries to bid against each other, for the privileges of our markets."[37] And if the United States can conduct an auction to see which of those countries is allowed in, it is not too far a stretch to say that it can decide to keep foreign nations out in a textbook version of economic protectionism. Indeed, Professor Calvin Johnson's recent study of the matter concluded that here, as in so many other places, the Constitution means what it says, and says what it means:

> In the original debates over adoption of the Constitution, "regulation of commerce" was used, almost exclusively, as a cover of words for specific mercantilist proposals related to deep-water shipping and foreign trade. The Constitution was written before Adam Smith, laissez faire, and free trade came to dominate economic thinking and the Commerce Clause draws its original meaning from the preceding mercantilist tradition. All of the concrete programs intended to be forwarded by giving Congress the power to regulate commerce were restrictions on international trade giving subsidy or protection to favored domestic merchants or punishing imports or foreign producers. Neither trade with the Indians nor interstate commerce shows up as a significant issue in the original debates.[38]

As Johnson's last sentence indicates, there is little or no historical evidence from the original debates as to the intended meaning of the Commerce Clause insofar as it applies to commerce among the several states. But there was clear, if regrettable, evidence that protectionism against foreign competition was one reason why Congress was given (and given first) power over foreign commerce. It seems very odd to think that the phrase "Congress shall have the power to regulate" has one meaning in dealing with foreign commerce and a distinct but narrower meaning with respect to domestic commerce when grammatically they apply the same way to both clauses. Hence, it does not make sense to assume that "regulation" in the Commerce Clause has its modern meaning of controlling wages, prices, and terms of trade for foreign commerce, but only the far narrower meaning for domestic commerce of allowing for the "regularization" of commerce by improving the structure of the commercial law, as by the use of writing requirements without any ability to override private agreements that fall within its scope. The modern meaning of "regulation" thus appears to apply in both contexts.

Given this background, it would be odd to take, as no one quite does, the extreme position that the power "to regulate commerce among the several states" works solely as an implicit limitation on state power, when the text is an explicit grant of power to Congress. In those cases where the Constitution's drafters wanted to impose explicit limitations on state power, they did so in separate provisions of Article I. Some of those imposed an absolute limitation on the power of states to do certain acts (e.g., enter treaties).[39] Yet other limitations allowed states to act only with the consent of Congress.[40] By all rights, if the Commerce Clause were meant to disable the states, it should be located with those provisions, which it is not. The sensible reading of the overall structure is one that speaks of a large federal power over interstate commerce, which is matched by a fear of state interference with it. It is just this sentiment that seems reflected when *The Federalist* noted how, in the absence of a union, commerce between the states would have been "fettered, interrupted and narrowed."[41] On this view it seems impossible as a matter of initial textual construction to read the Commerce Clause as though it were more important to limit the power of the states than to grant Congress any affirmative power.[42]

Those crosscurrents under the Commerce Clause did not reach the Supreme Court until *Gibbons v. Ogden* in 1824.[43] On balance, Chief Justice Marshall took the position that the clause gave substantial reach to federal power, but he did so in a context that cast the proponents of broad federal power into the virtuous role of defenders of free trade among the states. At issue in *Gibbons* was a New York state law under which Ogden (under an assignment from Robert Fulton) held an exclusive right to use steam power to run ferries between New Jersey and New York City.

The question was whether Ogden's New York exclusive franchise could block Gibbons, who held a federal coasting license, from plying the New York waters. Ogden argued that the commerce power allowed the United States to run only certain border checks of dubious utility, while leaving New York in exclusive charge of what happened on the waters interior to the state. Chief Justice Marshall would have none of this fantasy, holding that the power of Congress to regulate commerce among the states extended to all navigation of the journey from one state to another, even navigation that reached into the interior of the state. He further held, in ways that adumbrated the rise of the "dormant" or "negative" commerce clause, that the federal licensing statute was meant to preclude the creation of exclusive state franchises within state waters when commerce with other states was involved. Under the Constitution's Supremacy Clause, the state power to regulate in New York public waters had to give way when commerce from outside the state was involved. Purely state commerce, such as that on Lake George only, remained within the exclusive control of the states.

It is certainly easy to read Marshall's opinion as a celebration of federal power to curb the operation of state monopolies, for the broad reading of the Commerce Clause worked on those particular facts to create a unified and open national market in transportation. Yet one has to be aware of the limitations of that upbeat argument. Marshall in *Gibbons* was not concerned chiefly with free trade; to him, the main question was the scope of national power. Thus, one of the many arguments that he advanced to explain the broad scope of the commerce power rested on the sensible proposition that the word "commerce" as applied to commerce among the several states had to have the same meaning as the word "commerce" as applied to foreign commerce. He then noted that it was clear that navigation was subject to regulation in dealing with foreign commerce. He explained why thusly: "If commerce does not include navigation, the government of the Union has no direct power over that subject, and can make no law prescribing what shall constitute American vessels, or requiring that they shall be navigated by American seamen."[44] It is hard to imagine a more protectionist law. To illustrate that grand Marshallian ambivalence, suppose the tables had been turned and the United States had decided to award an exclusive franchise to Gibbons to ply boats between Elizabethtown, New Jersey, and New York City, while New York had sought to keep its waters open to all steamboat operators on that interstate run. Since the issue before Marshall was simply federal versus state power, one imagines he would have preferred the restrictive federal policy to the procompetitive state policy. National power, not economic competition, was his constitutional watchword.

In that sense, the next portion of the Marshall opinion is more important than the first. Marshall argued that the licensing statute implied that the federal government wanted to keep commerce open to all; thus, he relied on the Supremacy Clause to strike down the inconsistent state statute. But the conflict between the federal and state statutes was far from clear. The licensing statute could have been read as a nationwide certification of fitness to sail that did not preclude New York's local monopoly for steam power. But the strong pressures to block state interference with national commerce led Justice Johnson in his concurrence to assume that the Commerce Clause of its own force did preclude protectionist state regulation. In time, this view led to the adoption of the dormant commerce clause jurisprudence whose explicit, built-in *procompetitive* bias lasts to the present day. It quickly became established that—even when Congress chose not to act—the states could not enter areas that were reserved to the federal government, except with respect to local affairs. In *Brown v. Maryland*, Chief Justice Marshall struck down a state tax imposed on importers, for the privilege of doing business, on the ground that it was tantamount to a tax on the products imported.[45] There was little doubt in his mind that the Constitution limited the power of the states to tax imports, a response to the chaotic state of affairs under the old Articles of Confederation: "The oppressed and degraded state of commerce previous to the adoption of the constitution can scarcely be forgotten."[46] The creation of a national market free from state impediments seems an inexorable implication of a fundamental truth.

Yet once again the free-trade motif counts as only one of two themes. Larger, in fact, was Marshall's plea for congressional dominance over foreign commerce, as is evident in the sentence in *Brown* that follows the one just quoted: "It [commerce] was regulated by foreign nations with a single view to their own interests; and our disunited efforts to counteract their restrictions were rendered impotent by want of combination. Congress, indeed, possessed the power of making treaties; but the inability of the federal government to enforce them had become so apparent as to render that power in a great degree useless."[47] And Marshall in Gibbons relies on the parity between foreign and interstate commerce to show that both rely on the same definition of "commerce:"

> It has, we believe, been universally admitted, that these words comprehend every species of commercial intercourse between the United States and foreign nations. No sort of trade can be carried on between this country and any other, to which this power does not extend. It has been truly said, that commerce, as the word is used in the constitution, is a unit, every part of which is indicated by the term.
>
> If this be the admitted meaning of the word, in its application to foreign nations, it must carry the same meaning throughout the sentence, and remain a unit, unless there be some plain intelligible cause which alters it. [48]

Once again he held to the view that the meaning of the power to regulate commerce is the same in the domestic and foreign context. But in this instance, this tale at least has a happy ending, for the preemption of state laws fortunately vindicated the general principles of free trade, without any showing of a particular federal statute that was offended by the Maryland law. The basic contours of the dormant commerce clause were complete. The rest was detail.

One question that lingered after *Brown v. Maryland* was whether any area of transportation and trade was left to the presumptive power of the states. The first case to address that question was *Willson v. Black Bird Creek Marsh*, which recognized that Delaware was entitled to continue its program to drain a local marsh on what was regarded as a navigable waterway.[49] The use of the stream for navigation meant that state control over its operation was limited under the Commerce Clause, even when Congress had not legislated. *Willson* tempered federal power by introducing a balancing test by which the state could in some circumstances pass regulations under its police power in the event of federal silence.

Willson facilitates open competition between citizens of different states for two reasons. First, the maintenance of infrastructure is, in general, a government function. Second, the activity involved in this case did not distinguish between local and interstate commerce in order to hit the latter, as did the tax on importers struck down in *Brown*. But never forget that the theme of congressional dominance lurks in the background, for *Willson* signaled that the federal government could by explicit regulation preempt state legislation that served legitimate local functions. The balancing test protected state regulations against the dormant commerce clause but not affirmative exercises of congressional power.

Another question that remained was whether there were any strong local interests that allowed, or at least appeared to allow, local regulation to trump federal regulation. The most famous case on that topic was *Cooley v. Board of Wardens,* which upheld a Pennsylvania statute that required all boats in foreign and interstate commerce operating locally to employ a local pilot on the ground that his knowledge was necessary to secure local safety.[50] But, as so often proves the case, this ostensible safety argument was just pretext for the usual local anticompetitive preferences, for no safety statute would, as this did, allow a boat owner to opt out of the program so long as he paid half-pilotage to a fund for "the relief of distressed and decayed pilots, their widows and children."[51]

The Court accepted a dubious police-power justification to uphold local control in that case. In subsequent cases developing the dormant commerce clause, however, the Court tended to preserve open competition by allowing the state to assert its police power only against private activity that had serious adverse consequences for local interests. In the area of transportation, a representative decision is *Southern Pacific Railroad v. Arizona,* where the dormant commerce clause was held to preclude the application of an Arizona safety statute that mandated strict limits on the length of trains running interstate routes.[52] The reconfiguration of trains at the border was a clear impediment to interstate commerce and the local safety justifications were thin, for there was little reason to think that railroad operations in Arizona were riskier than those in any other state, given the uniform track standards. In the area of transportation, the Court's balance fell very much within the classical liberal position of free trade across open borders. But in those cases where there were strong local variations in conditions, as on local roads, the safety concerns had greater weight, and more state regulation was rightly allowed—until the interstate highway program standardized the operations on the roads.[53]

The modern dormant commerce clause is not limited to transportation across state lines, but also applies to the importation of goods from out of state. The leading modern precedent is *Maine v. Taylor*, where the state sought to prevent the importation of live baitfish.[54] The Supreme Court held that "the strictest scrutiny" applied and upheld the ban on importation only because the state was able to show that parasites contained in foreign baitfish posed a serious threat to local fish populations.[55] The ban on importation was not designed to prevent economic competition but to prevent the occurrence of common-law public nuisances that could not be controlled by any lesser means. It is also worth noting that in this case no nondiscriminatory law could do the job since it was only foreign baitfish that posed the peril in question.

When the dust settles, therefore, we end up with a pretty sound set of rules that do a number of things simultaneously. They keep open the arteries of interstate commerce by refusing to allow states to give in to local preferences that might limit or distort competition. But these nondiscrimination rules are limited at least to this extent: if the local regime imposes foolish restrictions on insiders, then it can impose equally foolish restrictions on citizens of other states. This system is far from perfect, but it works a lot better than it might appear, for no local business has an obvious interest in preserving an inefficient system from which it receives no comparative advantage. The dormant commerce clause thus counts as a decided plus for the classical liberal position. The affirmative Commerce Clause has often been used in a way that advances the classical liberal position, but its broad grant of federal power to regulate could be turned in the opposite direction.

Here it is worth noting that the one sensible but measured expansion of the affirmative Commerce Clause took place in connection with the advent of the antitrust laws, which were directed to various actions intended to monopolize or cartelize particular products or labor markets. The most obvious situation to which these laws might apply is mergers between firms located in different states in order to create nationwide monopolies. Cartels could operate in similar fashion across state lines. The question is whether such actions fall under the scope of the commerce power at all. The account that Chief Justice Marshall offered in *Gibbons v. Ogden* does not quite do the job. Marshall's emphasis on the movement of goods and services across state borders does not cover an agreement to merge or form a cartel since neither of those actions shifts goods. Nor is this problem cured by the position of Justice Johnson, for his view that the Commerce Clause forbids certain forms of state regulation by its own force does not extend the scope of the federal power. He too limited the power to transportation and sales, which does not obviously permit the regulation of cartels.

On a narrow view, therefore, the Commerce Clause would reach only those efforts to monopolize or cartelize businesses that themselves involved interstate commerce, such as railroads and the cross-border shipment of goods. The prosecution of price fixing or monopolization would be left to the individual states. That position could create immense difficulties if, for example, individual mergers were subject to attack under the law of each state in which the merged firms did business. It is therefore not surprising that, after some twists and turns, the Old Court took the position that the Sherman Act and, later, other anti-trust laws, were within the scope of the commerce power on the ground that these private cooperative arrangements had "a substantial effect on nationwide economic activity." The original foray into this area came in *United States v. E.C. Knight Co.*,[56] where the Supreme Court rightly stated that manufacturing fell outside the scope of the commerce power but wrongly concluded that a merger of corporations that did business in New Jersey and Pennsylvania should be treated as manufacturing. That decision proved short-lived, however, for in *Addyston Pipe & Steel v. United States* the Court did apply the federal antitrust laws against a multistate price-fixing cartel among pipe manufacturers.[57] Shortly thereafter, in *Swift & Co. v. United States,* the Court upheld an injunction against cartel activities in the meatpacking industry.[58]

Thus, the justices on the Old Court allowed an expansion of the affirmative commerce power beyond the cases that were envisioned by Chief Justice Marshall in ways that took into account problems of social organization that were not envisioned at the founding. But, once again, it is critical to recall that the antitrust cases, at least on the issue of congressional power, were not rationalized on the ground of advancing the general cause of competition. Thus, the Court would have also found that Congress had acted within its power under Commerce Clause analysis if Congress had decided to place organized labor under the antitrust laws or, as indeed happened with labor and agricultural activities, had exempted activities from the scope of those laws' operation. Yet no one before 1937 thought that the difficult matters pertaining to interstate mergers or price-fixing arrangements that involved transactions in two or more states undercut the basic logic of *E.C. Knight.* Manufacturing was still regarded as an exclusively local subject.[59]

C. Economic Liberties and Property Rights

The second portion of the pre-Progressive legal regime concerned the protection of individual rights of property and contract. Here, the post–Civil War cases articulating the various protections contained in the Fourteenth Amendment track quite closely the standard set of classical liberal concerns. That can be shown with a brief look at three bodies of law concerning the "public interest," antitrust, and labor.

I

Affected with the Public Interest

One of the major challenges in the post–Civil War period was to decide when various forms of rate regulation were proper. The formula that was used to approach this problem—that rate regulations were permitted when the industry was "affected with the public interest"—does not leap out as reflecting a special concern with monopoly power. And although there were cases that invoked this doctrine but did not cover monopoly situations, most early regulations were directed toward the regulation of monopoly power. The emergence of large network industries like telephony, railroads, and electric power all raised the prospect of industries that could work most efficiently as a single firm, on the ground that the cost of producing additional units of output falls continuously over the relevant output range. Put simply, it is inefficient to build duplicate facilities to provide telephone, railroad, and electric power service. Yet to permit a single firm to charge what it will is to allow it to reap a monopoly return. The point is that competition in such services is inefficient, but supplanting it with an unregulated monopoly may turn out—the point is hotly disputed—to be no better.[60]

To forestall that result, American case law adopted the "affected-with-the-public-interest" doctrine from the early English cases, most notably the celebrated case of *Allnut v. Inglis*, which held that a customs house with a state monopoly could charge only a reasonable price for its services.[61] In that case the state monopoly was created for good institutional reasons. The English imposed a tax on imported goods, but not on goods transshipped through the country, for to do so would have been to lose the transit business to foreign ports. Because it was not practicable to segregate those goods if they could be stored in *any* warehouse, they were consigned for storage in special houses for transshipment. But if the owner of those facilities could charge what he pleased, then he could raise the rates to neutralize the tax benefit that was otherwise conferred. To stop this tactic, it was necessary only to figure out the charges levied by competitive houses in the general market for storage on imported goods and to use those figures as the frame of reference for the custom-house market.

After migrating to the American scene, the doctrine faced a more difficult problem, for the creation of a single network eliminates the comparative pricing elements that were available in the *Allnut* situation: there were no general warehouses that offered the needed and convenient baseline. Thus, the effort to restrict prices ran into major difficulties over which (rightly) there were protracted disputes. One possible approach was to set a rate base equal only to the invested capital that was used and usable in the business, which placed on the regulator the unenviable task of second-guessing lots of business decisions.[62] An alternative was to adopt a system that gave a return on all invested capital at a lower rate, because the element of market risk was no longer present.[63] But here the regulated firm has little incentive to make the best choices for its investment. There are other permutations that are possible in different industries, but for our purposes, the best answer is not relevant. The point here is that the classical liberal model takes the question of monopoly seriously. It is very hard to determine the right answer, and to this day there is no consensus on the matter.[64]

Yet amid such complications, one thing is clear: for competitive industries, there is no sensible rate regulation. Justice Sutherland articulated that position in the famous case of *New State Ice Co. v. Liebmann*, which arose when one ice company sought to enjoin a new firm from entering the ice business on the strength of an Oklahoma statute that restricted entry to firms that had acquired a certificate of public convenience and necessity.[65] Sutherland did not see the latent threat of monopoly in the ice business. Accordingly, he declined to treat it as a public utility, holding that the defendant's business "is a business as essentially private in its nature as the business of the grocer, the dairyman, the butcher, the baker, the shoemaker, or the tailor."[66] The Court struck down a statute that created a local monopoly on the simple ground that it interfered with the like liberty of others to engage in the same business.

To be sure, the forces of Progressivism lay in wait, as Justice Brandeis conjured up all sorts of reasons why the state legislature might think that the ice business was different from thousands of others that require extensive front-end investment and are subject to the vagaries of supply and demand. Brandeis wrapped that dubious economic logic around a federalism theme that is meant to appeal to defenders of small government and decentralized power:

> There must be power in the States and the Nation to remould, through experimentation, our economic practices and institutions to meet changing social and economic needs. I cannot believe that the framers of the Fourteenth Amendment, or the States which ratified it, intended to deprive us of the power to correct the evils of technological unemployment and excess productive capacity which have attended progress in the useful arts. To stay experimentation in things social and economic is a grave responsibility. Denial of the right to experiment may be fraught with serious consequences to the Nation. It is one of the happy incidents of the federal system that a single courageous State may, if its citizens choose, serve as a laboratory; and try novel social and economic experiments without risk to the rest of the country.[67]

Yet this argument misfires in this context. There is little question that competition among states for the optimal structure of taxation and criminal law helps to check the state's monopoly power within its territory. But the entire Fourteenth Amendment rested on the assumption that states did not always confine themselves to these necessary activities. The need to restrain state power directed against individuals was apparent enough from the history of slavery, but was not limited to such cases: it arose in any case in which individuals were told they could not operate businesses within state borders.

Here, the one lesson we should have learned is the danger of state monopolies. The dormant commerce clause may stop discrimination against outsiders who are obvious targets in local political processes. But powerful insiders can restrict the trading options of local and out-of-state firms alike. Even though some experiments may be undertaken "without risk to the rest of the country," that is cold comfort to the local businesses that bear the state monopoly brunt with no choice but to pull up stakes. The claim of occupational and business liberty is a strong reason to preserve competitive processes from state domination within any given state. So too is the recognition that anyone who leaves the state has to abandon his local good will and other associational advantages. The exit right is an important safeguard against government power, but it is not a cure-all.[68] It is for that reason that ordinary businesses were not regarded as being "affected with the public interest." Would that we had that understanding today!

2
Antitrust Laws

The case for rate regulation stems from the belief that in certain network industries, with declining cost structures, a single firm can supply the market more efficiently than a group of competing firms. But in other cases, particularly involving cartels, the risk of monopoly comes from the cooperative behavior of firms unrelated to any social concern for efficiency. A strong libertarian has little use for antitrust law, because combinations in restraint of trade involve no threat of force or fraud against third persons. But a classical liberal, who takes his cue from Adam Smith's distaste for monopoly,[69] does not regard a cartel as just another form of contract. Rather, he treats cartels as presumptively illegal because in raising prices and lowering output they diminish social utility. Finding the right remedy is not an easy task. The standard English response, which has much to commend it, was to simply refuse to enforce various contracts that were thought to be in restraint of trade, while allowing those that worked not only to the benefit of the parties but also to the public at large.[70] In these cases, the chosen remedy was to deem the contract void, and thus unenforceable between the parties. In some cases, however, it is possible to justify cooperative arrangements among rival firms because they actually facilitate consumer welfare: check-clearing services among rival banks have that characteristic, for example. At

41

bottom, however, creating some regulatory regime to deal with monopoly power should not be regarded as necessarily, or even presumptively, off-limits.

Nor was it by the Old Court. The Sherman Antitrust Act was opposed on many grounds, including the absence of congressional authority under the Commerce Clause, but arguments that it violated a liberty protected by the Fourteenth Amendment were ignored.[71] Cartels were deemed "coercive," and even if that is not quite the right word to describe them, the basic point remains:[72] there is nothing about the theory of liberty of contract that rules all antitrust considerations out of bounds. As with rate regulation, the execution of that conclusion is fraught with difficulties left unaddressed here. But the key point to note is that the effort to fashion a coherent antitrust policy is not a fool's errand.

3
Labor Regulation

The last of our three headings concerns state efforts to regulate certain classes of employment contracts. Classical liberal theory is reasonably clear in its opposition to such regulations. The argument is that the freedom of both sides is compromised when laws limit the ability of the employer to exact some condition from prospective employees, or the reverse. That view does not necessarily call for the invalidation of all laws that deal with the regulation of contract, but it rightly asks the state to offer some justification for the restriction in question. Here the justifications of fraud, duress, and infancy are certainly available. But of those, the first two are of limited relevance: after all, it is hard to either deceive or coerce a worker into returning to the same job day in and day out. And even if there were some misunderstanding at the outset of the relationship, over time the expectations on both sides would become stable.

That leaves infancy or child labor as a state's rationale for restrictions. In principle, this question is difficult for there is little case for state intervention on matters of child labor if the parents are regarded as faithful agents of their children. Indeed, the prohibition on child labor often misunderstood the complex nature of these contracts, which often included, in addition to employment, some education and custodial care. The cost of invalidating these contracts was that it reduced the opportunities available to children who were members of well-functioning families. Although there are two sides to this issue on the merits, the matter never reached constitutional proportions. I am aware of no Supreme Court decision that invoked the liberty interest under the Due Process Clause to strike down any child labor statute designed to protect the youngest and most vulnerable of the population, even if child labor was rapidly giving way in a period with a rising standard of living.[73]

The justices of the Old Court did not take so kindly to other forms of regulation. It is important to note, however, that the Progressives overstated their case when they argued that those justices gave absolute and unswerving devotion to the principle of freedom of contract. As noted earlier, on the other side of the ledger stands the police power, which represents the inherent power of the state to protect the "health, safety, morals or general welfare" of the population at large.

Ernst Freund, perhaps the greatest combination lawyer and political scientist of his generation, began his magisterial 1904 treatise on the police power by defining it "as meaning the power of promoting the public welfare by restraining and regulating the use of liberty and property."[74] It deserves emphasis that the term "police power" appears nowhere in the Constitution but was read into the Constitution from the earliest times as an implied limitation on individual rights of property and contract.[75] Understanding it correctly is an enormous challenge, for this one reference points to, but does not define, the entire set of permissible justifications for state action. No classical liberal account can do without some version of the police power, which patterns the public law on the private law. The private law recognizes that individual rights of action against others are limited to protecting oneself or third parties, and the police power can be read consistently with this view. The term "police" picks up the need to restrain force and fraud by collective actions in the many cases in which private rights of action, whether for damages or injunctions, are insufficient.

The great challenge of constitutional law is to read the police power broadly enough to allow for the maintenance of social order, without allowing it to swallow the full set of individual rights that receive explicit constitutional protection.[76] The Progressives seized on the admitted need for some police power to argue that just about every form of state regulation was permissible. But more limited readings are much more persuasive. In principle, there is no doubt that the police power should cover those cases in which an individual, acting alone or in combination with others, causes harm to a third person, where *harm* tracks the meaning it has in the tort law—damage to person, chattels, or reputation—but does not extend to such matters as ordinary competition. To deny the police power in these situations is to put an end not only to the law of tort but also to the ability of the state to counter various nuisances so widespread and diffuse that private actions are unable to stop them, given the inability to isolate a single culpable defendant. But the case for extending the police power is more difficult when the harms in question arise out of an employment relationship, for now the consent of the worker is one reason to leave the loss where it falls, unless it is shifted in whole or in part by contract.

Yet it is important to note that, historically, the Constitution was read only intermittently to block legislation thus extending the police power. Various statutes aimed at protecting workers by limiting or striking down the assumption-of-risk or fellow-servant rules were routinely sustained during the early years of the twentieth century.[77] Similar provisions in the Federal Employers' Liability Act (FELA), which abolished these defenses as applied to the railroads, were upheld as well.[78] Thus, Justice Van Devanter followed well-established precedent when he wrote in 1912 that,

> A person has no property, no vested interest, in any rule of the common law. That is only one of the forms of municipal law, and is no more sacred than any other. Rights of property which have been created by the common law cannot be taken away without due process; but the law itself, as a rule of conduct, may be changed at the will . . . of the legislature, unless prevented by constitutional limitations.[79]

Justice Pitney expressed similar sentiments four years later in *New York Central Railroad v. White*.[80] What is striking about that approach is the level of leeway it allows to government, for there is no hint as to which constitutional limitations might prevent the legislature from acting at will, or why. Tested at the extreme, this proposition makes no sense, for if all rules of liability could operate at the whim of the state, then the state prospectively could repeal its laws against deliberate trespass and end private property as we know it. Any satisfactory application of the police-power principle, therefore, has to limit the scope of legislation. It is one thing, for example, to

46

repeal the laws of trespass and quite another to make the modest shift from a system of negligence to strict liability for accidental intrusions, when both sets of rules protect property against all deliberate and most accidental invasions. The one set of rules (strict liability in my view) may be better than the other, but the shift between them has only minor consequences for the survival of the institution of private property.

In the cases to which Van Devanter referred, the stakes were high given the heavy toll of railroad accidents. There is no question that employee health and safety issues were raised by the tort rules that were modified under FELA, and on this score there was much deference to the legislature—too much in my view, given the interest-group politics that could lead to the adoption or rejection of certain rules. Workers' compensation schemes, for example, tended to favor large firms that could spread the costs of the new regime over their entire work force, and many of those firms had adopted such programs voluntarily before the passage of the statute.[81] Thus, their support for the statute could easily be understood as an effort to raise rivals' costs, not to promote social efficiency.

Whatever the soundness of the Old Court's view on the scope of the police power as it related to tort law, the Progressives had no objection to the actual pattern of Supreme Court cases on the matter. The real controversy arose in connection with the maximum hour and minimum wage laws. With those, the issue before the Court was whether such statutes should be regarded as legitimate health measures, under the police power, or as "labor" measures, which fell outside the police power—indeed, whose chief objective was often to stifle competition for the protection of established industries and their privileged workers.

The famous, or infamous, 1905 decision in *Lochner v. New York* asked only whether a state law limiting bakers to a 10-hour workday was a genuine health measure or was instead a disguised "labor" regulation.[82] The opinion contains many references to the dangers of legislative paternalism, but a second, if tacit, dimension of the case concerns the competitive position of small, immigrant-owned bakeries against their larger, unionized rivals. Justice Peckham held that the safety issues were in fact a pretext for hobbling those workers, and it surely counts as a clear point in his favor that the case arose from a state criminal prosecution, and not from any private suit by Lochner's bakers. To be sure, Justice Harlan, who had pronounced libertarian leanings, dissented in the case on the ground that the health issues were paramount, giving no real analysis of the effect the hours limitation might have on the competitive balance.[83] Yet three years later, in *Adair v. United States*, he proved faithful to the old distinction between health and labor statutes; when the question arose whether the United States could require railroad employers to engage in collective bargaining with their workers, he took the strong position that this labor statute—for the health issues had dropped out of the picture—was an unacceptable limitation on freedom of contract.[84]

Adair was followed by a similar decision in *Coppage v. Kansas* in which Justice Pitney struck down a state collective bargaining statute for the same reason.[85] Indeed, acting as a common-law judge in *Hitchman Coal & Coke Co. v. Mitchell*, he carried his analysis of labor markets one step further by enforcing the standard "yellow-dog contract" that required a worker not to be a union member (or not to become one on the union demand) so long as he remained in the employ of the firm.[86] The key advantage of that contract from a social perspective is that it retards the formation of labor monopolies. Since the workers are in breach of their employment contracts so long as they remain on the job while having thrown their lot in with the union, the union has committed the tort of inducing a breach of contract by asking them to both stay on the job and be union members. With a yellow-dog contract in place, however, instead of having to bring countless (and futile) actions against individual employees, an employer could seek a single labor injunction against the union, a far more efficient process, while allowing those workers who are dissatisfied with the firm to quit first if they want to organize. Under the yellow-dog contract, the sole demand on the workers is that they display loyalty to the firm so long as they are in its employ. That duty of loyalty— that actions are taken for the benefit of the employer and not some other party—is uniformly recognized today for ordinary workers within the firm as well as for its corporate directors. Indeed, it is even recognized for certain key employees (e.g., workers with access to personnel files) in today's union environment.[87] The Old Court's application of the older common-law rule showed that on those issues the Court was more sympathetic to the preservation of competitive processes than its Progressive opposition, which failed to see the gridlock and dangers that could come out of its preferred system of labor legislation.

In sum, a fair assessment of the Old Court finds it allowing state action to control standard tort-like externalities, and even trumping the common law with respect to industrial accidents. But the Court's distinction between health and labor laws was not idle. It was strictly essential if state regulation was not to disrupt the operation of ordinary competitive labor markets, which Progressives viewed with such hostility and disdain. On the proper regulation of liberty and property, the justices of the Old Court did not get everything picture-perfect. Indeed, if anything they gave too much leeway to state police power by allowing state regulation in cases in which contracts could work well, and by their willingness to disallow employers the assumption-of-risk defense in many industrial accident cases. But by and large, their instincts were sound. The modern innovations in industrialization in no way required the abandonment of the old common-law rules so long as free entry was allowed on both sides of labor and product markets.

Progressives were wrong to focus on the size of an individual firm, wrongly perceiving large size as giving the employer the upper hand. They ignored alternative sources of employment, which created the upward pressure on wages that was observed in this period. To the Old Court dealing with matters of personal liberty, only tortious harm and monopoly were appropriate subjects of regulation. The substantive commitment to competition that received erratic affirmation under the Commerce Clause received fuller protection here as the Court blocked states that intruded on competitive markets by restricting liberty and property rights.

⤙ 3 ⤚

The Progressive Era

The Progressives took dead aim at many of the key decisions of the Old Court. To put the tension in perspective, it is critical to remember that no justice of the Supreme Court has ever held that all forms of state regulation are unconstitutional. In some areas, such as nuisance-prevention, there was little difference between the two sides, so the acid tests came elsewhere, chiefly in those areas in which Progressives attacked the two doctrines that most limited the scope of government power—federalism, on one hand, and the protection of individual liberty and private property, on the other. Although they ultimately prevailed on both fronts, they and their ideas come out second best as an intellectual matter. However grandly their rhetoric spoke about the need for sensible government intervention in response to changed conditions, the bottom line, sadly, was always the same: replace competitive processes, by hook or by crook, with state-run cartels. As before, I will begin with the federalism issues and then move on to the regulation of economic behavior.

A. Federalism Revisited

As shown earlier, the Commerce Clause, on its terms, does not require Congress to adopt only those forms of regulation that advance the operation of competitive markets. But within the traditional system, the authority of Congress to impose cartel-like arrangements on various industries was limited by the reach of Congress's power under the clause. Even when purely local commerce within any given state was in direct competition with interstate activity, the inability of the federal government under *Gibbons v. Ogden* to reach that commerce allowed for a certain welcome level of competitiveness within the joints.[88] It was just this escape from federal regulation that spurred the Progressives to expand the scope of the Commerce Clause.

The initial expansion took place with the railroads, which operated as a complex network industry. The Interstate Commerce Act of 1887 respected the traditional limitations of the clause by regulating rates only on interstate runs.[89] But in *The Shreveport Rate Cases*, the Interstate Commerce Commission—acting beyond the scope of the statute, no less—took the position that the Commerce Clause allowed it to regulate intrastate lines that were in direct competition with interstate lines.[90] In agreeing with this conclusion, the Court crossed the line between force and competition that is so critical to classical liberal theory. As early as 1838, in *United States v. Coombs,* the Supreme Court adopted a "protective" principle for interstate commerce that allowed Congress to pass laws that protected ships in navigable waters, subject to the federal maritime power, from criminal attacks launched within the states.[91] Justice Story justified the statute on the ground that the Commerce Clause "extends to such acts, done on land, which interfere with, obstruct, or prevent the due exercise of the power to regulate commerce and navigation with foreign nations, and among the states."[92] *Coombs* resonates with the classical liberal position because protection against force is one of the prime functions of government. It would be difficult to maintain federal control over interstate commerce unless this power was recognized in the federal government, which is why no one on either side of the intellectual divide has ever complained about that decision.

Yet there is in this, as in so many other areas, a vast difference between protection and protectionism, where the latter refers exclusively to protection of established businesses from the loss of their competitive edge. Even here a further refinement is needed, because the tort of unfair competition works within classical liberal lines when the "unfairness" in the competition comes from false statements a defendant makes about the products of a plaintiff competitor,[93] or, even more egregiously, from disruption of his channels of distribution by the threat or use of force.[94] But the term "unfair" is sufficiently pliable that it can be easily unmoored from its connections to classical liberal theory to cover loss because competitors offer superior goods, lower prices, better terms, or some combination of those.

That form of competition was at stake in *The Shreveport Rate Cases,* where the lower rates charged by in-state carriers sparked the Interstate Commerce Commission into action. There is no question that the configuration of railroad lines could easily create local monopoly situations. The demand would support only one line between, say, Omaha and Des Moines, but many lines between San Francisco and Chicago. Thus, a shipper who went from one end point to the other had the ability to reduce rates by playing off one carrier against the next. But only one of those lines might run through Omaha, putting shippers from that location at a huge disadvantage because of their inability to find alternative routes. The upshot is that stiff competition in the long-haul market could lead to an inversion of prices so that more is paid for a short haul (where there is no competition) than for the long haul of which the short haul is a part. Clearly, this odd rate structure cannot be the result of cost-based pricing as occurs in ordinary competitive markets. It arises only from the monopoly power over the shorter route. One purpose of the original Interstate Commerce Act was to limit the power of railroads to charge high rates on short hauls by decreeing that these short-haul rates had to be lower than the long-haul rates of which they were a part.[95]

But the complex interactions in railroad rates involved more than the long-haul, short-haul problem addressed by the original Interstate Commerce Act. Interstate lines could also be subject to competition from rails located entirely within one state. *The Shreveport Rate Cases* presented just that situation. Many towns in east Texas were served from both Shreveport and Dallas, and the interstate rates were higher than those within the state. In his decision in the cases the proposition that Justice Hughes rejected was that "Congress is impotent to control the intrastate charges of an interstate carrier even to the extent necessary to prevent injurious discrimination against interstate traffic" in the form of lower rates. He concluded as follows:

> Congress is empowered to regulate,—that is, to provide the law for the government of interstate commerce; to enact 'all appropriate legislation' for its 'protection and advancement'; to adopt measures 'to promote its growth and insure its safety'; 'to foster, protect, control and restrain.' Its authority, extending to these interstate carriers as instruments of interstate commerce, necessarily embraces the right to control their operations in all matters having such a close and substantial relation to interstate traffic that the control is essential or appropriate to the security of that traffic, to the efficiency of

the interstate service, and to the maintenance of conditions under which interstate commerce may be conducted upon fair terms and without molestation or hindrance. As it is competent for Congress to legislate to these ends, unquestionably it may seek their attainment by requiring that the agencies of interstate commerce shall not be used in such manner as to cripple, retard or destroy it.[96]

The clear implication of this passage is that local competition can be suppressed insofar as it is necessary to preserve the desired rate structure for the interstate traffic. The danger of this position is apparent, for one way to check the advancement of monopoly power, here of the interstate line, is to insulate potential local competition from the national regulatory structure. The factual issue in *The Shreveport Rate Cases* was complicated because local Texas rates were in fact subject to regulation by the Texas Railroad Commission. But just as it is wise to have two firms work in competition with each other, so too is it wise to force two regulatory commissions to work in competition with each other, for the system that authorizes the lower rates will be more likely to garner the larger fraction of the traffic. There is no doubt that the anticompetitive side of *Gibbons* showed through in *The Shreveport Rate Cases*. The key move in *Shreveport* was to commandeer the very broad definition of "injury" and "harm"—which now covered competitive losses—to expand the scope of the Commerce Clause so that the purely interior traffic of any state was no longer beyond the reach of federal power. The upshot was that the federal power now gobbled up huge portions of the transportation grid that once lay beyond it.

Nor did the expansion of congressional control over interstate commerce stop there. Only a decade later, the Court removed the requirement that there be competition between the local railroad and some interstate runs. The Transportation Act of 1920[97] authorized comprehensive rate regulation over the entire railroad system, and its power was duly sustained by the Supreme Court in *Wisconsin Railroad Commission v. Chicago, Burlington & Quincy Railroad*.[98] The linkage between the expanded reading of the Commerce Clause and the extension of government monopoly to the intrastate competition seems complete in the railroad cases.

The same pattern came up in connection with another of the critical pre-1937 Commerce Clause cases, only here the outcome was rather different. In *Hammer v. Dagenhart*, the Court by a narrow 5-to-4 vote rebuffed the efforts of the United States to leverage its admitted power to regulate interstate commerce to reach matters of local manufacturing, which at that time were subject only to state regulation according to a principle in no way questioned by *The Shreveport Rate Cases*.[99] The statutory strategy was to choke off from national and foreign markets all goods made by firms that used, or whose affiliates used, labor of children below the age of 14. This statute put before ordinary firms this grim choice: if you want to ship goods and services beyond state lines, you have to comply with federal guidelines on child labor, not the lower age minimums of your home state (age 12 in North Carolina, where *Hammer* originated). What Congress could do with one problem, it could do, of course, in response to any other. The same strategy could thus be used to impose federal directives on maximum hours, minimum wages, unionization, or the like. Some firms might resist these impositions by forgoing access to national and international markets, but these would be a hearty few. Most firms could not face the ruinous losses of their out-of-state markets to obtain some marginal gain from using child labor, especially if other firms capitulated to the federal mandate.

In one sense, *Hammer* seems easy: if the power to regulate interstate commerce is broad and plenary, then this statute falls within it, even if it frustrates rather than facilitates interstate commerce. After all, the "only" thing that the statute threatens is to keep goods out of interstate commerce. Justice Holmes took this position in dissent on the ground that whatever fell into interstate commerce could be reached by the federal government no matter what the government's ulterior motive.[100] That view was rejected by a five-member majority of the Court, speaking through Justice Day, which saw in the proposal a scheme to undermine the structural separation the Constitution established between local and national regulation. The federal squeeze would override any independent state police-power regulation to the contrary, thereby undermining any competitive pressures between states.

For our purposes, what is important in *Hammer* is the light it sheds on the general principle of competition between states as a means to choose the optimal level of regulation and, I will add, taxation. The ability of firms to relocate across state lines limits the possibility of high rates of state taxation. Many states have removed their inheritance taxes, for example, because older citizens relocated into low-taxation states. Just as the ability to quit disciplines the firm, so the exit right helps discipline the appetite of state governments. The famous Tiebout hypothesis states that competition between local governments allows ordinary citizens to sort themselves into those communities that supply the public amenities that best suit their own particular needs.[101] High taxes and oppressive regulation send a strong signal to those who can relocate elsewhere. The situation is not perfect: owners of land cannot migrate to another jurisdiction with their land, which is why zoning laws can both expropriate wealth and exert such great influence over land-use patterns. And in some cases, states may fight back by imposing taxes on firms that seek to exit, which has been the unhappy fate of some insurance companies that have sought to withdraw from business in states that have imposed stringent forms of rate regulation.[102]

This Tiebout phenomenon was very much at work in the child-labor cases. The federal government's argument advanced by John W. Davis, a noted lawyer who 38 years later was to represent the states in *Brown v. Board of Education*,[103] took the position that state competition was an evil because it meant that the states with the most lenient child labor laws would be able to prevail over those with more restrictive laws.[104] The point is true, but the hard question is, why condemn the result? Here the argument has to be that child labor laws are needed in order to prevent parents from abusing their offspring. On this view, weak laws should be construed as a license to commit neglect and abuse, so that more stringent standards become an urgent necessity. But that judgment presupposes that most parents of limited means will place their own interests above those of their children, when the safer assumption is that parents will trade off their own interests with those of their children, typically enduring great personal sacrifice to help ensure that their children lead better lives. On this view, parents whose children engage in child labor are making the best of a bad situation. If so, then the alternative to child labor is not a life of education or leisure for the young. It could be begging, prostitution, or back-breaking work in the informal economy, without the benefit of any legal protection at all.

There is, in other words, no reason to posit, as the Progressives did, that state child labor laws represent a race to the bottom, which would be the case if state law insulated firms located within state borders from suits for pollution brought by persons injured in their person or property. On this score, the historical evidence cuts against Progressives, for they have no explanation as to why the percentage of children in the workforce declined consistently throughout the period before federal regulation of child labor. The simple explanation is that increased productivity meant that parents could now afford to invest more in forming the human capital of their children via education. The gains from child labor diminished in comparison with its costs. The theories of Adam Smith work rather well.

Unfortunately, no argument that stresses the slow but steady improvement could slow down the Progressive challenge, so long as one child of tender age continued to work. The Progressives championed child labor laws, and made *Hammer* one of their key targets. Writing in *The New Republic*, Felix Frankfurter concluded, without analysis, that Justice Holmes's dissent "had never been answered," but then correctly added that, if *Hammer* were rightly decided on federalism grounds, a tax on the shipment of goods in interstate commerce—intended to end child labor everywhere—had to suffer the same fate as the total prohibition in *Hammer*,[105] which is exactly what happened in the *Child Labor Tax Case* decided in 1922.[106] Yet once again Frankfurter could not resist the opportunity to criticize the Old Court because of excessive reliance "on eighteenth century conceptions of 'liberty' and 'equality.'"[107] For him, the unproblematic case for the child labor laws left only the instrumental question: was it better to go for a constitutional amendment or better to seek to strengthen the state laws—his preferred alternative—notwithstanding the competitive dynamic that worked against any state effort to toughen its child labor laws.

The importance of competitive federalism was brought into greater relief in the New Deal period when the Court was faced with major federal efforts to organize various markets, often under the banner of "fair" competition. The efforts were in one sense supremely misguided because they misunderstood the source of the difficulties that faced the United States during the 1930s, when much of the nation's misery was self-inflicted through two means. First, the passage in 1930 of the Smoot-Hawley tariff (a decidedly Republican confection) blocked needed imports and precipitated a round of retaliatory tariffs that only made basic matters worse.[108] Second, the sharp deflation in the currency played havoc with existing contracts, most notably with long-term loans, which now required the borrowers to pay back far more in real terms than they had received in the first instance. (If 50 cents will buy what once took a dollar, the borrower who owes $100 has to pay back in real terms the equivalent of $200.) Those two sources of dislocation could not be stopped by introducing codes of "fair" competition that set specific price and quality standards for various kinds of goods. Such codes offered some protection to the retailers in certain trades by setting minimum prices. But the uncertainty that was eliminated for one class of preferred traders was not a systematic reduction in uncertainty. It only made other merchants and traders shoulder the added market uncertainty.

Examples of the efforts to organize markets were the "codes of fair competition" that were introduced under the National Industrial Recovery Act[109] and developed by various boards. One such code was at issue in *A.L.A. Schechter Poultry Corp. v. United States*,[110] the Live Poultry Code for the New York area, which included provisions that guaranteed the 40-hour maximum workweek, a minimum wage, a prohibition on child labor, and the right of collective bargaining for butchers and other workers. The provisions applied to the slaughterhouse operators who took possession of the goods after they had been shipped in interstate commerce. Within 24 hours, those operators in turn routinely shipped their meat products in separate transactions to local butchers for sale in the consumer market. Among the trade restrictions in the local codes was a provision that required a given slaughterhouse to purchase an entire run of poultry, including any sick poultry. None of those provisions makes the slightest sense from an economic perspective, and indeed the requirement to accept sick birds could easily be regarded as removing one important check for consumer safety. Chief Justice Hughes struck down this code on the ground that it regulated the movement of meat and poultry after they had left interstate commerce. He noted that the chickens had been shipped in from out of state, but responded, so what? "When defendants had made their purchases, whether at the West Washington Market in New York City or at the railroad terminals serving the City, or elsewhere, the poultry was trucked to their slaughterhouses in Brooklyn for local disposition. The interstate transactions in relation to that poultry then ended."[III] An *intra*state movement of goods followed an *inter*state movement of goods. In effect the poultry became indistinguishable from any other goods on the local roads.

The key question is why this simple line of argument might be thought so naive. The position is no more complex than one that holds that individuals are in local commerce when they take cabs or trains to and from the airport. They enter interstate commerce when they enter the airport and return to local commerce when they leave. The transitions here are no more complicated than going from a home or business to a public sidewalk or street: we have all done it and survived. "Before," "during," and "after" are concepts that we can all get our heads around. And, they allow for the articulation of the relatively clear lines of responsibility so central to any sound administration of a two-tiered jurisdictional system. This sensible view of the subject did not stop federal regulation of food products as they wound their way through the interstate distribution system, but it did work wonders in stopping the larger manifestations of federal power over the entire process.

Yet the *Schechter* accommodation would not last, for as political pressures got stronger, the Court went to great pains to conclude in 1937 that the conception of commerce derived from *Gibbons*, which proved viable in 1935, no longer met the modern conditions of 1937. Here, the integrated nature of the economy led the Court, again speaking through Chief Justice Hughes in *NLRB v. Jones & Laughlin Steel Corp.*,[112] to uphold the National Labor Relations Act against a constitutional challenge that it lay outside the scope of Congress's federal power to regulate interstate commerce. The labor statutes required an employer to negotiate in good faith with a union that was able to secure a majority vote among the members of some administratively determined bargaining group. Yet, no one could claim that any of those transactions took place "in" interstate commerce. The older conceptual scheme did not collapse of its own weight. All that really happened was that several justices lost faith in it, without being able to show where it broke down.

The same ruthless reading of the Commerce Clause took place in connection with agricultural arrangements, which are also amenable to state regulation. Here, the great ambition of the New Deal was to set and maintain prices for farmers well above the world level in order to protect the "right" of farmers to farm on terms they found congenial or, to be precise, to keep the domestic price of wheat at $1.16 per bushel when the world price was $0.40.[113] It is hard today to recall the Herculean effort that was needed then to keep the domestic prices of agricultural products far above world prices. To be sure, the ability to regulate the prices at which goods could be shipped in interstate or international traffic gave the United States a head start on this program of aggressive subsidies. But the foodstuffs that could not be shipped in international or interstate commerce could be shipped in intrastate commerce. This source of supplies would therefore undercut any effort by the United States to keep prices high. So the effort had to be made to make sure that other outlets for sale or use did not upset the grand plan. In *United States v. Wrightwood Dairy Co.*, decided in 1942, the Court took the first step and held that Congress could restrict the sale of dairy products in intrastate commerce because of the obvious effect that the sales would have on the price of goods in interstate commerce.[114]

Yet once again it is clear that even this strategy will not suffice against the countermeasures available to those intent on beating the system. After all, if the price for foodstuffs is kept artificially high by restricting the quantities available for sale, then it pays to *consume* any expanded output that is worth more than it costs to produce. So, Roscoe Filburn adopted just that strategy, which put him on a collision course with the Department of Agriculture that resulted in the decisive confrontation of *Wickard v. Filburn*,[115] also handed down in 1942. The Agricultural Adjustment

Act of 1938 limited the amount of crops that all farmers could grow in order to limit the output and raise the price of that which remained. Filburn produced twice the allowable number of bushels and was duly fined $0.49 for each of the unsold 239 bushels that were produced (for his own use) over the federal quota. He protested the fine on the ground that the Department of Agriculture had the power to regulate only distribution, not production. But the integrated nature of the overall market led Justice Jackson, previously Roosevelt's attorney general, to extend the heated logic of *Wrightwood Dairy Co.* one step further, so that Filburn's act of feeding grain to his cows became subject to Congress's power to regulate commerce with foreign nations and among the several states.

No one can doubt the extensive economic interdependence between local and national markets. Such had doubtless been the case, albeit on a reduced scale, from the founding of the Republic—the Roman Republic, that is. Yet if these effects are, and always were, self-evident, the desirability of *Wrightwood Dairy* and *Wickard* requires further analysis. Why should any court want to extend the scope of the commerce power beyond where Chief Justice Marshall had left it in order to expand a nationwide cartel, especially at a time when Thurman Arnold[116] was engaged in a hyperactive program of trust-busting that could only be justified (but certainly not in all its details) on the ground that competition was preferable to monopoly for reasons long familiar to economists?

One set of explanations is that this was not really an expansion of the Commerce Clause at all. Rather, the argument was that this was simply a return to the grand wisdom of *Gibbons* where the rationale behind the case was said to be far broader than the actual holding. Justice Jackson certainly took that line in *Wickard*, when he claimed that Chief Justice Marshall "described the federal commerce power with a breadth never yet exceeded."[117] One pillar for that argument is that Marshall described the power as "plenary," which it was, but only in the domain to which it extended.[118] At this point Justice Jackson took a page from the prose of Chief Justice Stone in *Wrightwood Dairy,* which noted that the commerce power "extends to those activities intrastate which so affect interstate commerce" as to make their regulation an appropriate use of the commerce power.[119]

Chief Justice Marshall had used similar words, but with an entirely different import from that attributed to him here. He did not speak of how far the commerce power "extends," but said the exact opposite: "Comprehensive as the word 'among' is, it may very properly be *restricted* to *that* commerce which concerns more States than one."[120] His entire point was that some *commerce* was exclusively intrastate, and thus beyond the power of Congress to regulate. Moreover, he had no intention whatsoever of claiming that any manufacturing or agriculture was covered by the power. All of that is sheer modern invention.

The same can be said of yet another effort to prop up the rickety intellectual foundations of *Wrightwood Dairy* and *Wickard*. That effort is an appeal to the Necessary and Proper Clause, which is less expansive than is commonly supposed. As drafted, the clause confers on Congress the power "to make all Laws which shall be necessary and proper for carrying into Execution the foregoing Powers, and all other Powers vested by this Constitution in the Government of the United States, or in any Department or Officer thereof."[121] Justice Jackson in *Wickard* briefly invokes the clause as an additional ground for a broad reading, but never analyzes either its text or the Marshall opinion.[122] Both cut clearly against the Jackson view.

The clause does not confer any new functions on Congress, but only makes sure that Congress has the means necessary and proper for carrying out the powers or ends authorized to it under some other clause. There is complete and total power over shipments in interstate commerce even if one does not regulate agricultural produce at its source. There has long been some uneasiness over whether Congress's power of "regulation" includes the ability to "prohibit" all goods of a certain type from entering into interstate commerce. It took the 5-to-4 decision in *Champion v. Ames* to uphold the power of Congress to keep lottery tickets out of interstate commerce even though they caused no damage to anyone while en route.[123]

But no one at the time supposed that this decision allowed Congress to regulate the manufacture of those tickets or even their local use. The same limitation to the Necessary and Proper Clause applied here. There is no need to regulate production or consumption to have plenary power over transportation.

The precedents cut the same way. The common view holds that Marshall gave an expansive reading of the Necessary and Proper Clause in *McCulloch v. Maryland*.[124] Instead of asking first whether a measure was necessary, and then if it were proper, he collapsed the two terms into the single word "appropriate," which surely expanded their meaning. But less well recognized is that Marshall did not use his overblown definition of necessary and proper at any point in *Gibbons*. His reference to the clause in *Gibbons* takes an entirely different line. There he says that "this limitation on the means which may be used, is not extended to the powers which are conferred."[125] This view makes it clear that the clause does not deal with the ends of congressional power, such that the Necessary and Proper Clause could extend the objects that were subject to congressional power. What he was anxious to do was show that any limitation that the clause placed on the means open to Congress did not matter in this case, which was concerned solely with ends. That view has to be correct, because any broad reading of the Necessary and Proper Clause—one that expands the ends Congress may pursue—makes pointless the entire system of enumerated powers of which the Necessary and Proper Clause is the last.

The textual and historical arguments, then, lay bare the claim that the Progressive reading of the Commerce Clause only returned us to the original Eden. So, we are back to the question: why move heaven and Earth to invent an imaginary Eden so that Congress could ensure the higher prices and restricted output characteristic of cartels? Note the inconsistent policies. Under the antitrust laws, the United States was prepared to spend public resources in order to *forestall* the creation of private monopolies and cartels (often overshooting in the process because of the government's failure to understand the procompetitive nature of certain practices, such as many tie-ins or exclusive dealing contracts). It then becomes passing strange that the federal government should also be prepared to expend public resources to *create* and *maintain* cartels. Make no mistake about it, most farmers were quite happy to yield to these general restrictions because they were the beneficiaries of the higher prices that the program generated for them at public expense.

Unfortunately, the Progressive intellectuals–turned–New Dealers did not have that excuse. Their mission was always to operate in the public interest. Yet their tunnel vision let them focus their attention exclusively on the beneficiaries of their programs, be they union members or farmers, while taking no note of the adverse effects that their programs had on the parties excluded from the market or forced to pay the higher prices that government policies maintained.

The manifest irony here is that the same intellectuals who attacked the members of the Old Court because of their narrow and prescientific point of view were guilty of a massive disregard of the basic established principles of economics that were well known to Adam Smith and David Ricardo. Those principles were trampled by the mercantilist impulses of the day. No judgment about social welfare can be made simply by celebrating the gains to one preferred group. A complete social analysis must look at all the effects, negative and positive. Any program that works like a cartel makes sure that one group gets a larger share of a smaller pie from which it may profit in the long run (although long-term profitability could easily be impaired as others seek to evade legal restrictions). But the situation is always a double disaster for those individuals whom regulation leaves with a smaller share of a smaller pie.

The decisive criticism of the Progressive program, then, does not depend on any exaggerated sense of individualism—of the 18th century or of more modern vintage. It depends on an overall programmatic critique that examines the effect that policy initiatives have on the full range of relevant parties. The only programs that should survive are those that produce some *net* social improvement. Accordingly, there is no good sense in saying that one bad program justifies a second, any more than there is in insisting on making a second hole in the bottom of a boat instead of patching the first. Yet that is what happened under the Progressive regime where one bad turn justified a second. The workers whom the Progressives reflexively supported on matters of employment suffered under the agricultural regimes imposed to benefit dairy and wheat farmers, just as those farmers suffered from the legal regime that the Progressives adopted for labor unions. Neither error cancels out the other. Rather, the two errors compound each other. The intellectuals who scoffed at Adam Smith and his archaic conceptions of liberty fell into the timeless traps about which he so eloquently warned.

The Court's Commerce Clause jurisprudence thus represents a dubious textual reading for an antisocial political end. The language of the clause is contorted so "commerce" now includes the home consumption that everyone took to be its verbal opposite. Politically, this tour-de-force of constitutional interpretation was justified by an ostensible social need to inject the federal government into problems too big to be left to the states. But so long as market liberalization is the path toward a rational agricultural and labor policy, the Progressive vision of American constitutionalism continues to prop up the most dubious of federal institutions.

To be sure, since 1995 the Supreme Court under the leadership of the late Chief Justice Rehnquist has beat a modest retreat from the commerce power's high-water mark. A bare majority of the Court has even purported to return to the fundamentals of the Commerce Clause by stressing the distinction between a Constitution with few and enumerated powers and one that gives the national government full sway over all human activities. Writing first in *United States v. Lopez*,[126] and thereafter in *United States v. Morrison*,[127] Chief Justice Rehnquist reiterated every sound general proposition about original constitutional structure and purpose. But, neither decision has done anything to unravel the Progressive vision that was so wholeheartedly embraced in *Wickard*. Rather, both cases nibbled about the edges of federal constitutional law to remove the textual embarrassment that comes from being unable to find *any* local activity that lies outside the capacious folds of the Commerce Clause. In *Lopez*, the Court struck down the Gun-Free School Zones Act of 1990 that made it a federal criminal offense "for any individual knowingly to possess a firearm at a place that the individual knows, or has reasonable cause to believe, is a school zone"[128]—that is, to possess a firearm within 1,000 feet of a school. Little of substance changed because a Texas law covered similar ground. Likewise, in *Morrison* the Court struck down a provision of the Violence Against Women Act, which made it, in essence, a federal crime to commit a dormitory rape— conduct that again was manifestly illegal under state law.

Unfortunately, Rehnquist's limiting principle, which was expressly and repeatedly affirmed, has had the perverse effect of solidifying the cartel-friendly logic of *Wickard*. Guns near schools and sexual violence in dormitories are said to fall outside the scope of the federal commerce power because they are fundamentally "noneconomic" in character—and, in addition, do not have, to invoke the standard phrase, any "substantial effect" on interstate commerce. By contrast, the agricultural regulation in *Wickard* was said to fall within the commerce power because the local activities regulated had a "substantial effect" on interstate commerce, even if they were not part of it.

The argument does not cut it. To be sure, the language of "substantial effect" had some sensible role to play in Commerce Clause cases even before the New Deal revolution. It was used to allow the antitrust laws to reach nationwide price fixing by corporations that did business in several states; as noted above, that represents a sensible extension of the original *Gibbons* rule that in no way invited or required the further inference that manufacturing or agriculture was uniformly subject to federal regulatory power.[129] That test is also used today as a *shield* under the foreign Commerce Clause to protect American consumers against foreign cartels that intend to, and do, rig our domestic markets.[130] But the foreign commerce power is also invoked as a *sword* under the 1918 Webb Pomerene Act, a national disgrace, to allow the United States to rig the price of American exports in international markets.[131] That line between manufacturing and antitrust seems clear enough and was maintained without difficulty in the pre-1937 period. Our Commerce

Clause is itself quite imperfect. But the Progressive vision of the Constitution has only made it worse.

B. Individual Rights

The second half of the argument requires us to recanvass the individual rights issues previously addressed by the Old Court that involved the doctrine of businesses "affected with the public interest," the antitrust laws, the controversy that surrounded wage-and-hour laws, and the entire question of labor unions, plus a new element that had not been much at issue in the Old Court—the protection of civil liberties in areas of speech and religion against novel forms of government action. On balance, the verdict is decidedly negative, as the penchant in favor of state monopolies and cartels that drove the Progressive decisions on federal powers often carried over to that area. The Old Court's mixture of broad liberties and limited police power works far better, and the Progressives come out best on the few occasions when they couch their arguments in an intellectual framework they generally discarded.

I
Affected with the Public Interest

One of the first major casualties of the Progressive revolution was the traditional rule that allowed price regulation only in those industries that were in some sense "affected with the public interest." Before the

Progressive era, the doctrine was largely but not exclusively tied to the regulation of natural monopolies. But the turmoil that arose during the 1930s led to the emphatic rejection of this doctrine in the pre-1937 decision of *Nebbia v. New York*.[132] At issue in that case was a minimum-price regulation that required all retail outlets in New York State to charge at least $0.09 for a quart of milk but did not in any way guarantee minimum rates to dairy farmers who bore the brunt of the excess capacity. Nebbia's criminal act was to sell milk for below the statutory minimum rate. The Court upheld the statute by expressing its agnosticism between competition and state monopoly as a way of doing business. Justice Owen J. Roberts first confessed his general "incompetence" to pass on the "wisdom" of various economic matters, and then demonstrated the truth of that proposition by offering this rationale to prop up the dairy cartel:

> The lawmaking bodies have in the past endeavored to promote free competition by laws aimed at trusts and monopolies. The consequent interference with private property and freedom of contract has not availed with the courts to set these enactments aside as denying due process. Where the public interest was deemed to require the fixing of minimum prices, that expedient has been sustained. If the lawmaking body concludes that an industry's practices make unrestricted competition an inadequate safeguard of the consumer's interests, produce waste harmful to the public, threaten ultimately to cut off the supply of a commodity needed by the public,

or portend the destruction of the industry itself, then any appropriate statutes passed in an honest effort to correct those threats may not be set aside because the new regulations fix prices reasonably deemed by the legislature to be fair to those engaged in the industry and to the consuming public.[133]

This brief passage has all the buzzwords about destructive competition and harm to consumers. In one of its inevitable findings, the legislature also noted that its new regime was supposed to eliminate a "menace to the public health,"[134] which could be said equally of any monopoly. But what it lacks is even the feeblest effort to explain how legislatures can determine a "fair" price for various commodities by principles that they are unable to announce or to explain to the courts. It is hard to see what set of circumstances would lead to the conclusion that courts should be indifferent to the creation or elimination of monopoly. The great vice here is that the legislature could not think of any reason to allow any dairy business to fail, so it turned cartwheels to make sure that others bore the brunt of this excess capacity. There is much that can be said against Justice McReynolds generally, including his willingness to go along with the prosecutions of *Schenck, Abrams,* and, especially, Eugene Debs in the aftermath of the First World War.[135] But those criticisms should not deflect attention from the soundness of his dissent in *Nebbia*, where in colorful language he rightly castigates the majority for failing to see that contracts normally result in mutual gain. "To him with less than 9 cents [this statute] says: You cannot procure a quart of milk from the grocer although he is anxious to accept what you can pay and the demands of your household are urgent! A superabundance; but no child can purchase from a willing storekeeper below the figure appointed by three men at headquarters!"[136]

Why is this so difficult to understand? Mercifully, Justice Roberts's attitude, expressed in his opinion for the Court in *Nebbia*, has not carried over to legislative efforts, draped in similar language, to impose differential taxes on out-of-state milk in order to discourage any disruption of the local monopoly power.[137] To this date, we have no explanation of how the same court that can relentlessly dissect the anticompetitive effects of overtaxation of foreign business cannot see that the same perils lurk in local rules that perpetuate cartels. The common explanation for this distinction is that the local citizens have better access to and greater sway over local politics than do outsiders, so the decision to police federalism issues is consistent with the more relaxed hand on disputes that are internal to the states. But that view makes a black-and-white distinction concerning what is at most a difference in degree. To be sure, it may be more likely that out-of-state interests will lose because they cannot voice their positions. But such a situation means only that there are fewer occasions in which local individuals will bear the brunt of statutes that deprive them of their liberty of contract.

There is no reason to rely on predictions of relative frequency when at the time of litigation the results are available for all to see. If a local statute prevents one firm from entering a line of business open to another, then we can assume that political clout worked its magic for one insider against another, as it often does in dairy cases. And, if a state statute treats outsiders even-handedly with local interests, there is no occasion for judicial intervention on their behalf. If local cartels are effectively forestalled by general rules, then the legislative process will change for the better, as no local interest will invest in legislation that cannot survive constitutional challenge. Stated otherwise, the same conceptual framework that works well to sort out cases involving individuals in different jurisdictions works as well for individuals within the same jurisdiction, so long as those local interests are subject to exclusion or differential treatment.

It is also critical to remember that the Progressives come out second best on their general argument that on matters of complex economic regulation the courts do not have the institutional competence to second-guess the legislature. Right now the Court gives a hard look at complex legislative schemes that are attacked on the ground that they are inconsistent with the dormant commerce clause. It also gives a hard look at complex systems of taxation that are challenged on the ground that their extraterritorial effects clash with the constitutional command that people should not be deprived of their property without due process of law. For example, in *American Trucking Associations v. Scheiner,* Justice Stevens struck down a Pennsylvania truck tax of $36 per axle, imposed on all Pennsylvania and out-of-state trucks, which did not vary with the mileage used, and hence with the damage caused to the local roads.[138] Thus, the tax fell disproportionately on out-of-state vehicles that were less likely to use Pennsylvania roads, on average, than their local competitors. Justice Stevens defended his conclusion with an accurate generalization that is worthy of Immanuel Kant's categorical imperative: "the tax must be such that, if applied in every jurisdiction, there would be no impermissible interference with free trade."[139] That is an accurate reflection of the sophisticated economic logic that underlies the decision. It asks whether any new distortions would be introduced into the system if other states followed the trail that Pennsylvania blazed. The axle tax would mean that each state would give its trucks the home court advantage. The errors would accumulate, not cancel out. The situation would degenerate into the pattern of retaliation feared by Chief Justice Marshall and brought into play with the Smoot-Hawley tariff.

The same kind of economic sophistication is brought into play when the legislation in question is challenged under the First Amendment on the ground that it infringes the freedom of speech or the free exercise of religion. Again the Court's jurisprudence in many instances follows classical liberal lines. Thus,

82

typically the Court looks for negative externalities—incitement to riot, commission of fraud—that justify government intervention. It also has applied the antitrust laws to the press notwithstanding the guarantees of freedom of speech. If it has the intellectual competence to work its way through such complex issues, then why is it utterly unable to apply the *identical* conceptual scheme to various forms of government regulation that are challenged on the grounds that they interfere with the liberty of contract or take private property, by way of coercive regulation, without just compensation? There is no theory of institutional competence that posits that the Court has great economic sophistication when it cares, but none when it does not. It requires no deep wisdom to see what is wrong with the legislation that was wrongly sustained in *Nebbia*. Competence has nothing to do with the matter. Every day, under the Sherman Act, the Clayton Act, the Telecommunications Act, and so on down the line, the Supreme Court routinely analyzes trade and business practices far more complex than the pathetic price-fixing scheme in *Nebbia*. The Court's flight to low-level rational basis review based on its own institutional incompetence lacks any firm intellectual foundation. Quite simply, it is not possible to marry any conception of limited constitutional governance with large doses of judicial passivity. The blunt truth is, the lower the Court's standard of judicial review, the weaker its intellectual performance. How could hard cases be decided correctly once the standard of constitutionality allows bad arguments to win, so long as uttered with a straight face?

2
Antitrust Laws

The Progressive response to the antitrust laws was to greet the laws in general with enthusiasm but to subject them to certain restrictions. The most important of these, the state action doctrine, reveals once again the Progressives' willingness to allow political institutions to impose state monopolies on competitive industries. Thus, in the watershed case of *Parker v. Brown*, the Court created an implied exception to the Sherman Act that exempted from antitrust enforcement California's raisin cartel because it was organized and maintained by the state.[140] The decision is quite perverse from every angle. The strongest case for not using the antitrust laws against cartels is that the administrative costs incurred by enforcement are not necessary because of the tendency of individual cartel members to cheat by secretly undercutting the cartel price in an effort to obtain larger shares. State cartel enforcement blocks this strategy, making the cartel more dangerous than ever; thus, federal antitrust law should apply with extra vigor against these state operations. Some deference to state activities might have been appropriate if the operation of the cartel were confined to California. But here the bulk of the cartel sales were out-of-state, which meant that consumers who did not participate in California's political process bore the brunt of its decision. Once the Commerce Clause reached those antitrust transactions, there was no reason to create an implied exception in favor of such dubious state policies.

The exemptions to the general antitrust law were not just implied. They were also express. In that regard, the most conspicuous portion of the Progressive platform was its deep conviction that the antitrust law should apply only to "ordinary" businesses, and not to the Progressives' two favored constituencies—farmers and laborers. The point was made crystal clear in the 1914 modifications of the Clayton Act, which exempted both labor unions and agricultural (and, for good measure, horticultural) activities from the operation of the statute, the former on the ground that labor is not an article of commerce and the second largely on the ground that agricultural produce is somehow immune from the ordinary rules of trade.

> The labor of a human being is not a commodity or article of commerce. Nothing contained in the antitrust laws shall be construed to forbid the existence and operation of labor, agricultural, or horticultural organizations, instituted for the purposes of mutual help, and not having capital stock or conducted for profit, or to forbid or restrain individual members of such organizations from lawfully carrying out the legitimate objects thereof; nor shall such organizations, or the members thereof, be held or construed to be illegal combinations or conspiracies in restraint of trade, under the antitrust laws.[141]

This statute shows all the indelible marks of special interest legislation, which at the very least leads one to ask what type of justification could be given in favor of this monopoly. There is surely no natural monopoly of the sort found in public utilities and network industries, which in any event are subject to explicit forms of rate regulation in which courts walk the tightrope of balancing the need to control monopoly behavior against the risk of rates so low that they effectively confiscate the investment of the firm's shareholders and creditors.[142] Nor do labor and agricultural monopolies create any incentive to produce new inventions or literary works, which is why the Constitution contains an explicit authorization for the federal protection of patents and copyrights, albeit only for limited terms. Yet no cartel has managed to be the source of any innovation. In some cases, the traditional labor statutes have been justified on the ground that they introduce a form of labor organization that is more efficient, unlike the common-law rules outlined above, which refused to require any system of collective bargaining. That position has been advanced most notably by Richard Freeman and James Medoff, who claim that the intervention of a third-party union creates bargaining efficiencies by mediating the relationship between the firm and the worker, which thus improves morale and working conditions within the firm.[143]

Yet, the argument is flawed from just about any angle. As a general theoretical matter, if the firm is made better off when its workers are represented in unions, then why do firms resist unionization so fiercely? One possibility is that they do not know their own interests. But if so, then who does? Do, for example, workers know their interests when asked to determine, before voting, whether union membership leaves them better off, net of dues and uncertainty, than they would have been without union representation? The willingness of so many workers to sign yellow-dog contracts suggests that some workers believe they are not better off with union representation. Whether one thinks that any of these decisions is proper from a social perspective is always a fair question. But it is not acceptable to take a position that selectively assumes that workers can make intelligent decisions on whether to accept a union while management cannot grasp that it is in its own interest to be shackled by a union.

Further evidence that unions can hurt the firms with which they deal comes from one key decision of the Progressive Era that tested the limits of section 6 of the Clayton Act set out above.[144] At issue in *Duplex Printing Press Co. v. Deering* was a massive union-led attack on one firm within the industry that remained a holdout against unionization.[145] Had the case involved only the firm's workers, everyone agreed that section 6 and section 20 of the Clayton Act would have protected the union from antitrust sanctions.[146] But the unions in that case mounted a full-court press that involved additional pressures on suppliers, transport firms, repair shops, customers, and others. Their motivation was simple. The large printing-press business had four major firms, three of which had been unionized. But, two of the unionized firms were restless and announced that they would terminate their union deals unless the Duplex firm was also subject to a union contract.[147] Hence the determined effort to force that last firm to capitulate through collective refusals to deal, which are paradigmatic violations of the Sherman Act if not covered by the antitrust exemptions of the Clayton Act. The question of statutory construction is quite close, and there was much to be said for Justice Pitney's position, expressed in his majority opinion, that limited the Clayton Act's union exemption to workers within a given firm.

If the function of unions is as Freeman and Medoff describe, the pattern of behavior observed in *Duplex* is inexplicable. After all, if unions have a positive function in improving worker relations, they have no need to engage in combined activities to improve their overall market position. Simple cooperation with individual employers should suffice. On the facts of *Duplex*, each of the three unionized firms should have announced with glee that it was eager to keep on with union relations because of the competitive advantage that unionization conferred on them against the nonunionized firm. Their combined resistance, however, makes clear what is common knowledge in any event. Unions are the most complex of monopoly organizations. Like ordinary monopolists,

88

as sellers of labor, they seek to raise wages and to lower their overall output to sustain that increase. But unlike the usual firm, unions face complex issues of internal governance that lead them to demand specialized work rules to protect individual members from displacement. Those rules are needed to keep the winning coalition together because unions, unlike firms, have no capital structure (whereby all workers own common stock in the enterprise) that transforms the maximum gain to the union into the maximum gain for its individual members. The inference seems inescapable that the exemptions from the antitrust laws had one and only one function: to preserve and advance union monopoly power.

3
Labor Regulation

The antitrust issues just discussed offer a useful segue to the Progressive view of labor regulation, much of which was developed in reaction to the *Lochner* decision on maximum-hour laws and the decisions in *Adair v. United States*,[148] *Coppage v. Kansas*,[149] and *Hitchman Coal & Coke Co. v. Mitchell*,[150] which dealt with matters of union organization. On both these fronts, the Progressive predilection for protectionism and monopolization becomes all too evident. Here again it is impossible to review all the cases that sustained various forms of regulation of the labor market, but it is instructive to examine at least a few.

One place to begin is with the well-known decision of *Muller v. Oregon*, which sustained the constitutionality of a statute that limited only women laundry workers to a maximum of 10 hours per day.[151] The attack on the statute rested on one simple proposition: "Women, within the meaning of both the state and Federal constitutions, are persons and citizens, and as such are entitled to all the privileges and immunities therein provided, and are as competent to contract with reference to their labor as are men."[152] The decision upheld the statute, citing the inferiority of women as a justification for the additional protection the law provides:

> The two sexes differ in structure of body, in the functions to be performed by each, in the amount of physical strength, in the capacity for long-continued labor, particularly when done standing, the influence of vigorous health upon the future well-being of the race, the self-reliance which enables one to assert full rights, and in the capacity to maintain the struggle for subsistence. This difference justifies a difference in legislation and upholds that which is designed to compensate for some of the burdens which rest upon her.[153]

It is worth noting, of course, that the architect of the detailed sociological studies used to justify this differential legislation was none other than Louis Brandeis, writing strongly within the Progressive tradition. On this issue, it seems clear that the modern feminist has rightly cast her lot with the libertarian. Differences in aptitudes and abilities there may well be, but this hardly justifies a set of public restrictions on the occupational choices open to women. The case resembles *Bradwell v. Illinois*, which famously took the position that differences in the physical and mental composition of men and women justified the exclusion of women from the practice of law.[154] But the key point here is not whether these differences do or do not exist or whether, if they do, their origin is in nature or nurture. Rather, whatever the differences, they should in an unregulated market be reflected in the occupations that men and women take in their effort to improve their own position. But, to take a leaf from the antipaternalist position of *Lochner* that is so often denigrated, the matter is not really the business of the state. If a woman finds the work too stressful, then she can switch to other lines of employment that better reflect her interests. But the choice is rightly hers, which she can make even if the huge majority of women take a different course—so long, of course, as they can find a willing employer.

Although Brandeis was happy to ply the Court with a sociological disquisition, that attitude did not survive, for it is easy to understand the element of economic protectionism involved in those statutes under which "laws justified as protecting women have been a central means of oppressing them."[155] It would be idle to assume that the transformation is complete, however, because the sex discrimination statutes today are routinely read to treat women as a protected class, even though one consequence of this muted form of protectionism is to make employers somewhat more reluctant to hire them in the first place. The classical liberal position here does far better precisely because its acceptance of the principle of formal equality reduces sharply the dangers of protectionism, while posing no threat, of course, to any program of voluntary affirmative action that a firm adopts with respect to sex or race or, indeed, anything else.

The attitude that proved so receptive to state regulation in *Muller* reached its apex nearly three decades later in *West Coast Hotel Co. v. Parrish*, which in one sense completed the mission that *Muller* had started.[156] At issue in the case was a violation of a minimum wage statute that applied only to women. In principle, *West Coast Hotel* was distinguishable from *Muller* on the ground that hours statutes relate to health because they concern levels of fatigue. Wage statutes, however, do not relate to the conditions of employment and thus look more like "labor" and less like "health" statutes. But, against this doctrinal objection, Chief Justice Hughes offered two rejoinders, both unsatisfactory.

First, he noted that "[t]he Legislature was entitled to adopt measures to reduce the evils of the 'sweating system,' the exploiting of workers at wages so low as to be insufficient to meet the bare cost of living, thus making their very helplessness the occasion of a most injurious competition."[157] Once again, exploitation was presumed rather than demonstrated, and competition was understood only as a force that led to the bidding down of wages, never to their bidding up.

Second, he claimed that "the denial of a living wage" also "casts a direct burden for [women's] support upon the community."[158] The definition of a living wage is not supplied, and the presumed dislocations never demonstrated. Nor does the argument inquire into any of the increased burdens that might fall on the community if other effects of minimum wage laws are taken into account: the dismissal of some employees, the reconfiguration of employees' working hours and conditions in ways that make it more difficult for them to care for their families at home, and the inability to land an initial job from which orderly advancement is possible. But for all Chief Justice Hughes's efforts, *West Coast Hotel* no longer represents the law today insofar is it carves out a special place for women. The ostensible solicitude for the position of women is subject to the same objection that may be lodged against the statute in *Muller*: it excludes women from jobs they would prefer to take relative to any other available.

The wages and hours legislation was not, of course, the only arena in which the Old Court was forced to give ground. Most critically, the cause of collective bargaining that had been resisted by the Old Court slowly gained ground through the passage of both the Norris-LaGuardia Act in March 1932 and the National Labor Relations Act of 1935, each of which operated from the fundamental premises of the Progressive worldview, which accorded the entire practice well-nigh mystical power. Felix Frankfurter defended the cause as follows in the pages of the *Yale Review*:

"Collective bargaining" is the starting point of the solution and not the solution itself. This principle must, of course, receive ungrudging acceptance. It is nothing but belated recognition of economic facts—that the era of romantic individualism is no more. These are not days of Hans Sachs, the village cobbler and artist, man and meistersinger. We are confronted with mass production and mass producers; the individual, in his industrial relations, but a cog in the great collectivity. The collectivity must be represented and must be allowed to choose its representatives. And it is through the collectivity, through enlisting its will and its wisdom, that the necessary increase in production alone will come. Needless energy is wasted, precious time is lost, precious feelings are diverted and disturbed by the necessity of fighting for the acceptance of the principle of collective bargaining instead of working out the means and methods of its application.[59]

The statement repeats all the standard economic errors. It assumes that size matters more than market structure and that wages bear little relationship to productivity. Yet it forgets that wages rose and hours fell considerably under the legal regime that Frankfurter so disliked. And worst of all, it wants a blank check from the very firms and individuals who are sure to lose both flexibility and profitability under the labor scheme that he endorses, whose particulars he cannot specify. That system, however, was adopted under the National Labor Relations Act of 1935, whose statement of purposes posited a false relationship between increased productivity and increased unionization.[160] The key finding reads:

> The inequality of bargaining power between employees who do not possess full freedom of association or actual liberty of contract, and employers who are organized in the corporate or other forms of ownership association substantially burdens and affects the flow of commerce, and tends to aggravate recurrent business depressions, by depressing wage rates and the purchasing power of wage earners in industry and by preventing the stabilization of competitive wage rates and working conditions within and between industries.[161]

It is difficult to know where to begin in deconstructing a provision that animates our labor law to this very day. The use of the term "full" in the first sentence is an obvious effort to finesse the point that the common-law system gave all workers the same formal freedom that was possessed by employers, including the right to turn down one offer for a better one. Nor was there the slightest recognition that this one common-law right had led to major improvements in working conditions since the turn of the century, as indicated in the small set of statistics cited earlier.[162] Rather than face this implication head on, the finding seeks to locate a fundamental difference between the worker and the firm by noting that the use of the corporate form had allowed for the aggregation of wealth on only one side of the market. But the argument is wrong for three reasons.

First, there is nothing that prevents workers from voluntarily banding together to negotiate, subject to the usual restraints of the antitrust laws, which under the Old Court had been applied to them in the same manner as to firms.[163]

Second, nothing about the corporate form of association suggests that firms that have not violated the antitrust laws have any degree of market power. It is yet another application of the same error that pervades Progressive thought, of confusing firm size with market power without recognizing that employer-side cartels are hard to create, given that many workers can easily take their skills into different industries.

Third, there is no credible explanation why the same employment practices that worked in the boom years of the 1920s had anything to do with the downturn of the 1930s, which is much more clearly traceable, as noted earlier, to two events unrelated to labor markets: the passage of the Smoot-Hawley tariff and the rapid deflation of the currency. Nor do unions counteract any of the baleful effects of a depression. The wage increases that are granted to protected workers necessarily reduce the money available to pay wages to their nonunionized rivals. So once again the statement stresses the desirable effects to a subset of the population while ignoring the undesirable effects imposed on those workers who fall outside the ambit of statutory protection.

Moreover, the nice reference to the stabilization of wages reveals that same error and a covert motive. The only way that wages can be stabilized for one group is for others to bear the full brunt of exogenous market shocks. The motive for stabilization was the creation of cartel-like wages, which could only be sustained, owing to the ability of many workers to move across industries, if similar controls were imposed on all industries simultaneously. So when the dust settles, the usual neutral rationales in favor of collective bargaining turn out to be a cloak for the organization of monopoly power, under a system of complex collective bargaining rules that increase the risk of breakdown between the parties. More results are adverse consequences on third parties, such as the major disruptions in airlines and railroads, not to mention major league sports. The shutdown of the 2004–2005 National Hockey League season is an out-growth of the legal framework in which collective bargaining took place.

What is so impressive about the situation is that even this added measure of protection could not prop up the role of labor unions in private markets. The decline in private-sector unionization is an oft-remarked-upon phenomenon, with union member-ship dropping from close to 35 percent at its peak in 1955 to around 8 percent today, including public-sector unions. I have little doubt that this figure would be still lower if firms had the right to deal or not deal with unions as they saw fit. This decline cannot be attributed to any recent changes in the law, for in this area, at least, the basic doctrines have scarcely changed in the past 40 or so years, and what changes have occurred have not tended to switch the balance much in either direction, unlike the employment anti-discrimination laws that have moved sharply in one direction since their adoption in 1964. Rather, the explanation comes from other sources.

First, a good defense can, in general, beat a good offense. The firm that understands that disgruntled workers tend to form unions will take steps to keep them pleased. The *causes célèbres* for union organization are just not there. Second, the nature of industry has continued to evolve and is marked by an ever-increasing heterogeneity inside the workforce, so that it is difficult for workers with divergent interests to form a common alliance that works to their mutual advantage. Third, increased labor mobility, both within and across geographical regions, stymies union organization. The workers who think that they will be in a different location, different job, or different career in five years are much less willing to incur the heavy front-end costs of an organization campaign that, even if successful, will tend to benefit the next generation of workers. Fourth, and perhaps most important, no labor union can survive when tariff barriers no longer insulate it from global markets. Free trade means that each firm has a smaller share of the relevant market. Any effort to push up wages results in a more rapid flight of jobs to foreign suppliers that no amount of local pull can overcome.

The bottom line is that the only unions that have expanded their influence and scope are public-sector unions, because local governments have taken the position that they will not refuse union recognition so long as unions do not disrupt services through strikes. That supine practice counts as a breach of fiduciary duty by public officials, which means that taxpayers, many of whom are of more limited means than union members, have to shell out monopoly wages for no good reason. Calvin Coolidge, in a telegram to Samuel Gompers in 1919, was right when he said, as governor of Massachusetts, "there is no right to strike against the public safety by anybody, anywhere, any time." The need to curtail disruptions by strikes in other areas such as education is less imperative but nonetheless strong, and that cannot be achieved by allowing unionization when competitive markets can secure an appropriate public labor force.

There seems in the short run little reason to think that the status quo of strong public and ever weaker private unions will change. But for our purposes it is sufficient to note that the Progressive vision of industrial justice never did, and never could, live up to the exalted expectations that it would transform the workplace. The reason why competition is preferable to monopoly does not depend on the configuration of the labor force, the conditions of production, or wage levels at any given time. It depends on the view that the dynamic ability to mix and match individuals through voluntary transactions will create a high productivity–low transaction cost environment that differs markedly from the rigid, unresponsive firm structure that mandatory collective bargaining so frequently creates.

4
Civil Liberties: The New Challenge

Thus far I have talked about those issues of federalism and economic liberty that lay at the core of the Progressive movement. It would be a mistake, however, to end this discussion without casting an eye toward some of the civil liberty issues that first arose at that time. There is much to commend in the skeptical attitude that some leaders of the Progressive movement took toward government suppression of protest during wartime. On this score, the single most famous opinion is the justly praised opinion of Justice Holmes in *Abrams v. United States,* where he dissented from a decision upholding the criminal conviction of a group of Bolshevik sympathizers of anarchist or socialist tendencies.[164] Their crime was to have supported the new Soviet government that had signed a peace treaty with Germany, with whom we were then at war, on the supposition that these sympathizers might persuade munitions workers to go out on strike.

Here the debate was not over ends; for the continuity of industrial effort is critical in wartime. Instead, the issue is the familiar one that crops up in a thousand different settings: just what mix of frequency and severity of some potential harm allows the government to swing into action? The debate is by no means a simple choice between remedies before and after the fact. The clear and present danger test that Holmes made famous concedes that some anticipatory remedies are appropriate when the danger is both large and near at hand.[165] But the danger of overuse of state power means that the dominant lesson is that in most cases of public protest the government is less likely to err if it waits than if it plunges forward.[166] In urging caution against intervention, Holmes not only understood the need to balance two kinds of error but also asserted, with great rhetorical effect, that the forces of competition, routinely denounced as injurious or destructive, were better seen as the solution than the problem:

> But when men have realized that time has upset many fighting faiths, they may come to believe even more than they believe the very foundations of their own conduct that the ultimate good desired is better reached by free trade in ideas—that the best test of truth is the power of the thought to get itself accepted in the competition of the market, and that truth is the only ground upon which their wishes safely can be carried out.[167]

Indeed, any coherent version of the First Amendment requires that we recognize that the offense some people take to others' views cannot count as "destructive" competition simply because those others ask people to abandon established ideas in favor of some contrary, or even outlandish, position. Political risk, like economic risk, does not normally justify government control over private behavior.

Yet, for the most part, the Progressive movement cannot be seen as a blessing for civil liberties. Thus, note that virtually all the decisions that the Progressives championed relied on a limited conception of ordinary liberty and a broad conception of the police power. That mix proved toxic in *Plessy v. Ferguson*, which no one should take as a Progressive decision as such, but which rested on just that combination of factors. Only the first Justice Harlan dissented: he had libertarian inclinations that led him to restrict the scope of government action.[168] It is not quite an accident, therefore, that the resegregation of the U.S. Civil Service was brought about under a Progressive regime, that of Woodrow Wilson. His reasons made at least a verbal appeal to the broad police power that the Progressives championed. When Wilson resegregated most parts of the civil service he was "primarily inspired by the fear that blacks carried contagious diseases and secondarily moved by the feeling that blacks had become disrespectful to their white superiors."[169] As Charles Paul Freund writes: "Wilson's historical reputation is that of a far-sighted progressive. . . . Domestically, however, Wilson was a racist retrograde, one who attempted to engineer the diminution of both justice and democracy for

American blacks—who were enjoying little of either to begin with."[170] It would be incorrect to say that Progressives favored this maneuver, which many actively opposed. Rather, the reproach is that Progressives supported a strong conception of judicial quiescence, which made Wilson's actions possible. That clear legal position helps explain why the National Association for the Advancement of Colored People, which had been formed only in 1909, chose not to make a constitutional challenge to the government's decision. That challenge would have proved hopeless under *Plessy*. The deadly combination of a narrow conception of individual liberty and a broad conception of government police power (here, as it relates to the power of the federal government to operate its own affairs) ensured that this legislation would have withstood any challenge at the time.

In other civil rights settings, the blame can be laid much more squarely at the Progressives' doorstep. Thus, two of the Old Court decisions that remain in good graces today are *Meyer v. Nebraska*[171] and *Pierce v. Society of Sisters*,[172] both of which relied on a broad conception of liberty and narrow conception of the police power to limit state control over education in private schools, both religious and secular. It is important to recall just what these statutes required. In *Meyer*, the state sought to ban instruction in any foreign language of students who had not finished eighth grade. In *Pierce*, the restriction cut still deeper and prohibited parents from educating their children in private schools, religious or secular, if they were between the ages of 8 and 16. Lest one forget the state of mind that allowed these statutes to be sustained in lower courts, it is worth setting out the policy justification the Nebraska Supreme Court adopted in upholding the statute:

> The legislature had seen the baneful effects of permitting foreigners, who had taken residence in this country, to rear and educate their children in the language of their native land. The result of that condition was found to be inimical to our own safety. . . . The obvious purpose of this statute was that the English language should be and become the mother tongue of all children reared in this state. The enactment of such a statute comes reasonably within the police power of the state.[73]

The answer of Justice McReynolds relied squarely on the Due Process Clause of the Fourteenth Amendment to give a broad definition to liberty and a narrow conception to the police power:

> While this Court has not attempted to define with exactness the liberty thus guaranteed, the term has received much consideration and some of the included things have been definitely stated. Without doubt, it denotes not merely freedom from bodily restraint but also the right of the individual to contract, to engage in any of the common occupations of life, to acquire useful knowledge, to marry, establish a home and bring up children, to worship God according to the dictates of his own conscience, and generally to enjoy those

privileges long recognized at common law as essential to the orderly pursuit of happiness by free men.[174]

Justice McReynolds applied this logic to the more draconian restrictions at issue in *Pierce*:

> Under the doctrine of *Meyer v. Nebraska* we think it entirely plain that the Act of 1922 unreasonably interferes with the liberty of parents and guardians to direct the upbringing and education of children under their control. As often heretofore pointed out, rights guaranteed by the Constitution may not be abridged by legislation which has no reasonable relation to some purpose within the competency of the State. The fundamental theory of liberty upon which all governments in this Union repose excludes any general power of the State to standardize its children by forcing them to accept instruction from public teachers only. The child is not the mere creature of the State; those who nurture him and direct his destiny have the right, coupled with the high duty, to recognize and prepare him for additional obligations.[175]

It is worth noting that Justice Holmes dissented in *Meyer*, taking the same view of the scope of the police power that he took in *Lochner v. New York*. He wrote in the companion case striking down a similar statute in Iowa that it was only "with hesitation and unwillingness" that he disagreed with his colleagues, but he added that "if there are sections in the State where a child would hear only Polish or French or German spoken at home I am not prepared to say that it is unreasonable to provide that in his early years he shall hear and speak only English at school."[176] He concluded, in language that anticipates the Brandeis dissent in *Liebmann*, that "therefore I am unable to say that the Constitution of the United States prevents the experiment being tried."[177] To his credit, Holmes did not dissent in *Pierce*, although it is hard to see why his exceedingly deferential interpretation of the Due Process Clause would lead him to strike down a statute that was passed after evident deliberation, with the same strong asserted justifications as the statute in *Meyer*.

It is worth pondering, however, how these two decisions fit into the Progressive tradition. On this score, Felix Frankfurter once again makes the point unmistakably clear. Shortly after *Pierce* came down, he wrote an unsigned editorial in *The New Republic* titled "Can the Supreme Court Guarantee Toleration?"[178] Frankfurter had no brief for the statutes struck down in *Meyer* and *Pierce*, but his deep conviction about the narrow scope of liberty under the Due Process Clause led him to bite his lip and attack both decisions. Again, his words must be quoted to be believed.

> Before one can find in the Oregon case proof of the social value of the Supreme Court's scope of judicial review a balance must be struck of all the cases that have been decided under the Fourteenth Amendment. In rejoicing over the Nebraska and Oregon cases, we must not forget that a heavy price has to be paid for these occasional services to liberalism. The New York bakeshop case [*Lochner*], the validation of anti-trade

union laws, the sanctification of the injunction in labor cases, the veto of minimum wage legislation, are not wiped out by the Oregon decision. . . .

For ourselves, we regard the cost of this power of the Supreme Court on the whole as greater than its gains. After all, the hysteria and chauvinism that forbade the teaching of German in Nebraska schools may subside, and with its subsidence bring repeal of the silly measure; . . . But when the Supreme Court strikes down legislation directed against trade unions, or enshrines the labor injunction into the Constitution, or denies to women in industry the meagre protection of minimum wage legislation, we are faced with action more far-reaching, because "it is" ever so much more durable and authoritative than even the most mischievous of repealable state legislation.[179]

To his credit, Frankfurter accepted the indivisible notion of liberty and was prepared to stifle even meritorious claims to liberty to support his overarching program for the major economic issues of the day. Both his attitude and Holmes's had powerful consequences for the subsequent shape of the law. Thus, it is no accident that Holmes had some sympathy for the great Progressive cause of eugenics; his notorious decision in *Buck v. Bell* declared that "[t]hree generations of imbeciles are enough," and thus allowed the state to railroad a helpless woman of normal intelligence and poor background into forced sterilization.[180] Indeed, the evidence is clear that Holmes did not hide behind his usual veil of judicial restraint. He wrote: "It is better for all the world, if instead of waiting to execute degenerate offspring for crime, or to let them starve for their imbecility, society can prevent those who are manifestly unfit from continuing their kind."[180] After all, it is just one of those "hysterical laws," albeit one that lasted for more than 50 more years.[181]

And Justice Frankfurter carried forward his overarching views on the massive state power over education into the well-known flag-salute decision of *Minersville School District v. Gobitis*,[182] where, writing for the Court, he combined the dominant themes of the Progressive movement into a most unappetizing stew. Thus, in sustaining the power of the state to force Jehovah's witnesses to express allegiance to the flag in violation of their religious beliefs, he relied on the inability of courts to make judgments about the complex issues raised, only to make clear thereafter his collective vision of the world:

> The ultimate foundation of a free society is the binding tie of cohesive sentiment. Such a sentiment is fostered by all those agencies of the mind and spirit which may serve to gather up the traditions of a people, transmit them from generation to generation, and thereby create that continuity of a treasured common life which constitutes a civilization.[183]

That civilization survives by symbols all must accept. This view is about as far as we can go from the Lockean tradition of the social contract whereby individuals surrender some limited property and liberty in exchange for security but are free to act as they please so long as they do not inflict harm on their neighbors. What was still worse was Justice Frankfurter's utter inability to see that the coercive techniques that he tolerated bore an eerie similarity to the requirements of public fealty that typified the Nazi regimes with which we were soon to come into mortal conflict.

Fortunately, this was one portion of the Progressive agenda that did not last, for *Gobitis* was overturned only three years later in *West Virginia Board of Education v. Barnette*, where Justice Jackson showed a much livelier appreciation of the risks of state coercion.[184] He wrote: "If there is any fixed star in our constitutional constellation, it is that no official, high or petty, can prescribe what shall be orthodox in politics, nationalism, religion, or other matters of opinion or force citizens to confess by word or act their faith therein."[185] Justice Frankfurter remained unrepentant. He insisted that the "general libertarian" sentiments expressed by the majority did not establish valid constitutional norms. He retreated to the standard Progressive position that gave liberty a narrow construction, chiefly limited to preserving bodily integrity, and the police power a broad one, covering all ambitious social schemes.[186] He wrote: "I cannot bring my mind to believe that the 'liberty' secured by the Due Process Clause gives this Court authority to deny to the State of West Virginia the attainment of that which we all recognize as a legitimate legislative end, namely, the promotion of good citizenship, by employment of the means here chosen."[187] There is a steely consistency in Frankfurter's world view that acquits him of any charge of judicial opportunism. But he should stand indicted and convicted for bad judgment for abandoning judicial oversight of the political process. Whether the issue was economics, religion, or speech, constitutional protection remained at its low ebb under Progressive theories.

⁀ 4 ⁀

The Post-Progressive Period

The positions that many Progressives took on civil liberties, it seems fair to say, have been widely repudiated on both sides of the political spectrum— unless they are revived, as to date has not been the case, by the rising forces of social conservatism in the United States. Of critical importance is the form of that repudiation. One possibility was to keep the basic Progressive insight that all economic, religious, and social issues should be judged by the same standards when looked at through the prism of liberty as that term is used in the Due Process Clause. Under that view of the subject, the position of the Old Court returns to favor on economic matters, and carries over to issues of speech and religion as well. The basic presumption is that the police-power justification for state actions must be directed at some real evil and not some symbolic harm such as those the Progressives found persuasive in cases like *Meyer, Pierce, Gobitis*, and *Barnette*.

That, of course, is not what happened. Rather, the Progressive mindset has continued to dominate American law on the same economic issues to which Frankfurter attached the highest priority: unionization, wages and hours, and rate and price regulation. But a different attitude took hold on matters of speech, religion, and race. Indeed, it took virtually no time for the split to take place. Cases like *Meyer* and *Pierce* were reinterpreted to involve freedom of speech and religion under the First Amendment, which were, after all, the twin grounds on which Justice Jackson relied in *Barnette*. But the decision to repudiate the Progressive tradition only in part led to the great doctrinal divide that has dominated constitutional law to the present day. Thus, in *United States v. Carolene Products Co.*, Justice Stone examined an inane piece of protectionist legislation for the dairy industry in Wisconsin.[188] The decision upheld the law using the then-standard maneuvers that found the Commerce Clause was broad enough to sustain the statute, and the guarantees of individual rights were too puny to overturn it.

The magnitude of those maneuvers' impact, however, floored Justice Stone, who was concerned with cases that dealt with voting rights and racial discrimination, where the same attitude would require the Court to acquiesce in the mischief that segregation had worked in the South and allow the Frankfurter view to prevail on matters that involved religion and education. So, he sought to hedge his bets by allowing for, indeed inviting, the possibility of a constitutional recrudescence on those sensitive issues in famous footnote 4. Justice Stone wrote that any "specific prohibition" of the Bill of Rights could have bite against both the state and federal government.[189] These included religion and speech protections, but, as matters turned out, not protection of private property under the Takings Clause. That clause has real bite only in cases of physical occupation,[190] but not in cases involving land-use regulations, even those with a massively disproportionate impact.[191]

Stone then continued: "It is unnecessary to consider now whether legislation which restricts those political processes which can ordinarily be expected to bring about repeal of undesirable legislation, is to be subjected to more exacting judicial scrutiny under the general prohibitions of the Fourteenth Amendment than are most other types of legislation"—and quickly noted that the right to vote, the right to political expression, and the right to assembly could so count.[192] And last, he noted broadly: "Nor need we enquire whether similar considerations enter into the review of statutes directed at particular religious, *Pierce v. Society of Sisters*, or national, *Meyer v. Nebraska*, or racial minorities, whether prejudice against discrete and insular minorities may be a special condition, which tends seriously to curtail the operation of those political processes ordinarily to be relied upon to protect minorities, and which may call for a correspondingly more searching judicial inquiry."[193]

Indeed, if Congress and state legislatures always acted with the public interest at heart and always had perfect information, then each piece of legislation would count as a social improvement that would pass the most stringent standards of review imaginable. No law would produce more harm than good, and the general nature of the legislation would offer a strong guarantee that the gains from political action were spread more or less uniformly across the general population. There would be no reason to incur the high costs to police a just compensation requirement. But Justice Stone rightly perceived that the lumpiness of the political process could lead to situations where easily identifiable factions could be subject to exclusion from or marginalization in the political process, which certainly happened to blacks in the South and to Jehovah's Witnesses in Pennsylvania and West Virginia.

In sum, there is nothing wrong with Stone's instinct that the courts must intervene in those cases in which the political process breaks down. Nor is there any reason to quarrel with his view that the breakdown of the political process was most acute and least defensible in the areas of race and religion that he identified in *Carolene Products*. Without question, if the choice were to extend constitutional protection to the areas that Stone enumerated or to those involving economic rights, we should choose Stone's list in a heartbeat.

The question remains, however, why frame the issue of judicial oversight in this either/or form? If Stone is correct, then a set of *uniform* standards should make it more likely that judicial intervention will respond to the risks to discrete and insular minorities. Once we see the particulars of given legislation, it may be easy in other cases to conclude that the victims of oppressive legislation are large corporations that lack inside political clout. The chief mistake of Justice Stone was to assume that these perceived defects in the political process could only apply to certain kinds of issues or to certain sorts of classification. To be sure, it may be easier to organize discrimination against religious or racial groups. But the clever and determined legislature can, and often does, direct its power against other groups, such as businesses that operate from out-of-state, or landlords whose voting power is smaller than that possessed by tenants, or employers whose political clout is matched or exceeded by unions, or women whose political influence lags behind that of men.

Given the sorry history of economic protectionism, the key insight of the classical liberal position needs constant reaffirmation: there are no permanent good or bad guys etched into the political spectrum, so that legislation that introduces class bias or worse is possible along any number of dimensions, and often the highest sounding rationales conceal the basest forms of protectionist legislation that interfere with the operation of sound competitive principles in all areas of life. The correct approach, therefore, is to repudiate the Progressive tradition lock, stock, and barrel to the extent that it advocated, as it frequently did, judicial quiescence on a full range of economic, political, and social issues.

∽ 5 ∽

Progressivism Today

The central tenet of judicial deference on questions of property rights and economic liberties continues to work itself into the fabric of modern law. Stated in a nutshell, the history of the post-Progressive Era has largely been one in which the distinctions that were mentioned but not adopted in *Carolene Products* worked their way into the fabric of modern constitutional law as the Supreme Court has struggled, largely in vain, to explain why breakdowns in the political process in some areas deserve a higher level of judicial scrutiny than similar breakdowns in others. There have been in the past 20 years some modest cutbacks of the Progressive tradition as it applies to the Commerce Clause and economic issues. But these have been erratic and slight, and basically limited by the current crop of justices, whose ostensible retrenchment in *United States v. Lopez* starts from the assumption that *Wickard* represents good law, before nibbling around the edges.[194] The current dominance of the Progressive tradition in the areas of its prime concern—commerce and economic liberties—rests on two pillars. Some justices continue to follow it because they accept the Progressive synthesis and have no willingness to "turn the clock back," while others think that, although the original decisions were incorrect, the doctrine of *stare decisis* precludes any return to the sounder principles of an earlier era.

The picture with respect to the few cases that challenge legislative restrictions on economic liberties and property rights is somewhat more confused given the recent 2004 term, which featured three notable cases that revisited the questions of federal power, economic liberties, and private property that had been thought to be closed.

Gonzalez v. Raich[195] raised the question of whether the provisions of California's Compassionate Use Act[196] could survive given their manifest conflict with the federal Controlled Substances Act (CSA).[197] The former carved out an exception to the general drug-use prohibition, allowing individuals whose medical conditions required using naturally grown marijuana to alleviate pain to do so without running afoul of the law. The United States for its part treated marijuana as a highly dangerous substance that could only be used in restricted circumstances and explicitly rejected any compassionate use exception for individuals like plaintiffs Raich and Monson.[198] The plaintiffs clearly suffered from conditions that would warrant the use of marijuana under the California statute. To escape the clutches of the federal government regulating under the Commerce Clause, they sought systematically to sever all connections between their marijuana use and any economic activities inside or outside the state. Monson grew her own marijuana, and Raich was given the marijuana free of charge by another person who grew the supply in the state. Under the definitions of commerce that applied in *Gibbons v. Ogden,* there is little question that neither of those transactions involve commerce among the several states, and, in the case of Monson, any form of commerce at all.

The legal landscape, however, was dominated not by *Gibbons* but by *Wickard v. Filburn,* which held that feeding one's own grain to one's own cows counted as a form of commerce among the several states because of its effect on overall supply and price.[199] The same argument proved decisive in the opinion that Justice Stevens wrote for a six-member majority of the Court in *Raich.*

The Court said that it was not possible to look in isolation at the marijuana consumed by two individuals. Rather, the case depended on the influence that the total level of transfer and consumption had on the interstate supply from which it was not sealed off. In dealing with this effort, the Court adopted a well-nigh conclusive presumption that medical uses of marijuana could not be separated from common trafficking, and thus it allowed the government to rely on the grandiose statements of purpose that were included in the CSA in 1970.[200] In truth, there was some real evidence of abuses in the administration of the California program that supported this position.[201] But at no point did Justice Stevens ask whether the programs in other states were subject to similar abuses, or even contemplate the possibility that a tighter program could help individuals like Raich and Monson without opening the floodgates. In effect, he treated the general findings of the CSA as though they resolved all questions of fact in a manner that shows a marked difference in approach from *Lopez*. The three dissenters argued that *Lopez* covered the situation and, in the case of Justice Thomas,[202] that the modern jurisprudence of the Commerce Clause is hopelessly out of kilter.

The popular response to this decision was, in fact, divided and confused. The dominant sentiment was sympathy for the individual plaintiffs whose lives were at risk from the decision: the human interest side of the story dominated the federalism issues of the case. Ironically, none of the justices of the Supreme Court took seriously the contentions of the government that the medical usefulness of marijuana was fantasy.[203] The defenders of the decision took refuge, therefore, in the undisputed fact that the case was not a referendum on the soundness of medical marijuana. Any unhappy enforcement of the CSA is now a matter to be taken up with Congress, where the antimarijuana forces were (and are) ready to resist any relaxation of the overall standard. Lost in this shuffle were the virtues of federalism on a question of this sort. It seems clear that the scope of permissible uses of potentially dangerous drugs will not easily qualify as some kind of fundamental liberty that is protected by the Due Process or Equal Protection Clauses. There are too many potential complexities in the use of these products to be confident that they do not have serious adverse impacts on a class of unsuspecting users, or pose risks of increased harms to third persons.

But even if that point is conceded, one of the virtues of federalism, which the Progressives recognized, is that it does allow for some experimentation on questions of regulation.[204] In this case, the experiments do not sound far-fetched, because nine other states had programs similar to that of California.[205] The decision in *Raich* snuffed out those possibilities in circumstances where it is hard to see a dominant federal interest. All the states involved enforced marijuana prohibitions against local use (as if they were federal matters anyhow), and the federal government could strengthen its campaign against interstate shipments no matter which way *Raich* was decided. The popular unease with the decision is well supported by stronger legal argument. It now appears, however, that any further retreat from *Wickard* will depend on a change in composition of the Court.[206]

The two recent decisions on economic liberties and private property are every bit as instructive. In the first of these, *Lingle v. Chevron USA, Inc.*,[207] a unanimous

Supreme Court upheld the constitutionality of an uncommonly ugly Hawaii statute that had two major features.[208] First, it forbade major oil companies (all of which were from out of state) from raising rents or otherwise discharging their independent franchisees. Second, it stipulated that the major oil companies could not open up new outlets within one-eighth of a mile of an incumbent dealer in urban areas, or one-quarter of a mile in other areas. At trial, the testimony in the case was directed chiefly to the question of whether consumers were benefited or hurt by a statute that in effect insulated independent franchisees from the business control of their franchisers. But any effort to imagine some consumer benefit from so ill-conceived a statute willfully overlooks the blatant efforts of the local franchisees to protect themselves from economic competition in ways that hurt both the consumers and the major oil companies.

In the Supreme Court, Justice O'Connor, writing for a unanimous Court, spent her time worrying about verbal niceties that did not cut to the heart of the question. The lower courts had used a snippet from an earlier property case, *Agins v. City of Tiburon*,[209] in which the Supreme Court had said that the government regulation of private property "effects a taking if [such regulation] does not substantially advance legitimate state interests."[210] In a decision that showed scant interest in dealing with the substantive issues raised by the case, the Court recanted its earlier use of this test, "however fortuitously coined,"[211] in favor of the tripartite test that it developed in *Penn Central Transportation Co. v. New York City*,[212] which Justice Brennan had fashioned in order to uphold New York's landmark preservation statute against a charge that it took property without payment of just (indeed any) compensation. In somewhat despairing tones, Justice O'Connor wrote:

> The Court in *Penn Central* acknowledged that it had hitherto been "unable to develop any 'set formula'" for evaluating regulatory takings claims, but identified "several factors that have particular significance." Primary among those factors are "[t]he economic impact of the regulation on the claimant and, particularly, the extent to which the regulation has interfered with distinct investment-backed expectations." In addition, the "character of the governmental action"—for instance whether it amounts to a physical invasion or instead merely affects property interests through "some public program adjusting the benefits and burdens of economic life to promote the common good"—may be relevant in discerning whether a taking has occurred.[213]

Justice O'Connor has always shown a marked partiality toward balancing tests. But in this instance at least, her recitation of the *Penn Central* factors should not be taken as a sign of legal sophistication and candor. Rather, it should be understood as a confession of her inability to develop principled rules to decide concrete cases. But in fact the sprawling *Penn Central* test, while highly favorable to government in most cases, represents the kind of unprincipled ad hoc thinking that is so congruent with the Progressive Era. List a range of factors and refuse to acknowledge the role or relevance of any of them, and it is easy to conclude that the statute is constitutional.[214]

Matters are worse in that the factors listed are largely incoherent. The phrase "investment-backed expectations" has no discernible content and is by no means a synonym for the term "private property," which it replaces. Its sole function here is to insist, against an unbroken common-law tradition, that future development rights are not protected under the Takings Clause. Only existing uses are entitled to that protection, which creates an impossible conceptual tangle in the many cases where property of great economic value is presently unused and undeveloped. The "character of the government actions" is meant to draw a distinction between the outright occupation of land on the one hand and restrictions on the power to use or dispose of it on the other. But while that difference may surely be relevant to the question of how much compensation is owed, no explanation is given as to why it allows for a categorical distinction between property taken and property regulated. And the willingness to concede that it is all right for public programs to go about "adjusting the benefits and burdens of economic life to promote the common good" represents yet another illustration of the naïve optimism that infuses Progressive thought.[215]

The community is not understood as a collection of individuals, with the welfare of each important to the bottom line. Rather, property owners, whose wealth is rapidly diminished by a novel restriction of development, are treated as though they fall outside the community, so that their interests need not be taken into account at all. The adjustments contemplated allow for windfalls and wipeouts, without any guarantee that the former are larger than the latter or any effort to make those who benefit compensate those who are wiped out. There is, in other words, "no average reciprocity of advantage" that suggests that all individuals receive benefits in proportion to their losses, thereby providing some protection against the dangers of faction that Progressives too easily overlook.

One might think that tests that are so incoherent on their face should succumb under the weight of the most obvious of criticism. But in *Lingle,* Justice O'Connor took *Penn Central* as settled and sound law and sent the case back to lower courts for further consideration under *Penn Central,* where in all likelihood the regulation will be sustained on the ground that rent control legislation usually passes constitutional muster so long as the landlord is able to recover the costs of its operation. Unless there is some clear sense of what counts as right and wrong, the strong element of deference nurtured in the Progressive Era will continue to hold sway in property cases just as it did in economic liberty cases.

The public response to the *Lingle* decision was muted, for ordinary people frankly do not trouble themselves over the choice of verbal formulations that are used to test various forms of economic regulation. The same cannot be said, most emphatically, about a second takings case that was argued the same day as *Lingle* but which came down only at the end of the 2004 Supreme Court term. There have been few cases that have prompted as much of a public uproar as *Kelo v. City of New London*,[216] which offered a major test of the public responsiveness to the Progressive tradition in connection with the Takings Clause: "Nor shall private property be taken for public use, without just compensation."[217] Whereas *Lingle* had concerned the shadowy world of rate regulation and exclusive territorial provisions, *Kelo* hit people exactly where they lived: could the state take their homes in the name of general economic development?[218] When the Court announced in broad strokes that this could be done, it provoked all sorts of reactions, including legislative activity in Washington, D.C.; California; Illinois; and Texas, among other states, all with the common view that "we can't let *Kelo* happen here."

Here is how the melodrama started. The City of New London, Conn., which had long been an economically depressed community, conducted extensive public hearings that led to the adoption of a large-scale redevelopment plan that called for the destruction of a large number of private homes in the city to promote local economic development. There was no evidence of any corruption or bribery in the local process that might have triggered Progressive opposition. As a social matter, therefore, the case squarely evokes the Progressive image of a conflict between the welfare of the recalcitrant individual and that of the community at large. The obvious question in the case was whether land was in fact being taken for a public use when it would be conveyed to private developers to use as they pleased on ground leases that called for rent of a dollar per year. In fact, the actual facts of the case were far worse than this capsule account suggests, because the bumbling city planners at work already had at their disposal about 90 acres of publicly owned land that could be sold off for private development without knocking down a single home. Worse still, for all its endless deliberations, the city did not have any concrete proposals in place for construction projects on the publicly owned land.

As often happens, the market moves more rapidly than a tardy government project. The original conception was that the development should complement with fancy hotels and upscale office space the new Pfizer research facility that had been completed in 2000, five years before this case was decided. But the nearby suburban market had already responded to Pfizer's needs, so that the original projects were no longer viable. The houses were condemned largely as an adjunct to a failed project. Its designated purpose was for "park support," a term with no clear meaning to the planners who invoked it.

The unhappy particulars of this case did not stop Justice Stevens, writing for a five-member liberal majority (himself, Justices Souter, Ginsburg, and Breyer, and a reluctant Justice Kennedy), for he was prepared to throw in his lot with the planners, without worrying overmuch about what they had in mind. In taking that position, he relied on the oft-quoted language of Justice William O. Douglas in *Berman v. Parker*,[219] which praised the wisdom of government land planning even after the overall Progressive claims for centralized economic planning had already been discredited. At issue in that case was an urban renewal project in Washington, D.C., which targeted a "blighted" area of the city where Berman's department store was located. Berman challenged the condemnation of his property, claiming that it was not for a public use since his store itself was not blighted. None of that had the slightest effect on Justice Douglas, who wrote:

> We do not sit to determine whether a particular housing project is or is not desirable. The concept of the public welfare is broad and inclusive. The values it represents are spiritual as well as physical, aesthetic as well as monetary. It is within the power of the legislature to determine that the community should be beautiful as well as healthy, spacious as well as clean, well-balanced as well as carefully patrolled. In the present case, the Congress and its authorized agencies have made determinations that take into account a wide variety of values. It is not for us to reappraise them. If those who govern the District of Columbia decide that the Nation's Capital should be beautiful as well as sanitary, there is nothing in the Fifth Amendment that stands in the way.[220]

The clear message in this case is that the more extensive the government's intervention in land-use issues, the greater the social benefit that will follow. Justice Douglas writes as though a beautiful community can be guaranteed by a state decree. At no point did the risk of failure, let alone of faction and politics, enter into the equation. Yet these are ever present even in the construction of roads and court houses. The greater the scope of permissible government action, the higher the level of abuse, and the lower the possible return from public investment, which is typically funded by taxes exacted from others. But the good-government frame of mind allowed the Court to say that any lawful public purpose is sufficient to satisfy the public use requirement within the Takings Clause.

That hugely deferential frame of mind carried over into other cases. Most notorious on the list was the 1981 decision of the Michigan Supreme Court in *Poletown Neighborhood Council v. City of Detroit*,[221] which allowed the destruction of a large neighborhood of homes and shops for the construction of a new General Motors plant, which never could live up to the extravagant economic claims made on its behalf. The Michigan Supreme Court has finally repudiated that decision in *County of Wayne v. Hathcock*.[222] *Hathcock* favors a narrower rule that yields to earlier precedents by allowing, under the state constitution, and with obvious uneasiness, the condemnation of blighted properties while forbidding condemnation for general economic development.

The situation on the federal frontier, however, was decidedly different because Justice O'Connor, writing in 1984 for a unanimous court in *Hawaii Housing Authority v. Midkiff*,[223] stretched the concept of public use beyond its breaking point when she wrote that a taking satisfies the public purpose prong of the Takings Clause if it is "rationally related to a conceivable public purpose."[224] In a concurring opinion in *Kelo*, Justice Kennedy made explicit the connection between this standard and the Progressives' wholesale retreat on economic liberties, writing that "this deferential standard of review echoes the rational-basis test used to review economic regulation under the Due Process and Equal Protection Clauses."[225] Indeed, that hugely generous standard was strictly required by *Midkiff*, where the Court upheld a Hawaii law that allowed a tenant to ask the state to buy out the landlord's interest in property so long as the tenant put in escrow the money needed to fund that purpose.[226]

Justice Stevens conceded in *Kelo* that "it has long been accepted that a sovereign may not take the property of *A* for the sole purpose of transferring it to another private party *B*, even though *A* is paid just compensation.[227] So the question is, why did Justice O'Connor not find that side constraint violated in *Midkiff*? Easy when you have unlimited ingenuity. Simply hold that the concentrated landholdings in Hawaii, here in the hands of the powerful Bishop

Estate, constituted some form of "oligopoly" that the legislation was designed to relieve.[228] At this point the game is up: any land grab will be part of a comprehensive scheme that will have some indirect public benefit that renders the public-use language a dead letter. Simultaneously, this expansive view of public use just ignores the strategic behavior of the sitting tenants who profit from the scam.

Within that overheated framework it was still possible to find for Ms. Kelo and her fellow owners. No one claimed that the property was blighted; no one thought that these isolated homeowners occupied some oligopolistic fortress. And no case had ever held that ordinary private homes could be taken for a public purpose that had yet to be articulated at all. To Justice O'Connor, who distanced herself in dissent from her *Midkiff* opinion, *Kelo* represented the power of the rich and mighty to trample the interests of the little man.[229] And it is no irony that all four dissenters (Justices Rehnquist, O'Connor, Scalia, and Thomas) downed their sometime scruples about judicial restraint. Justices O'Connor and Thomas wrote powerfully that government excesses of this sort should not be tolerated if the public-use limitation is to survive the modern welfare state. The overall lesson here is too clear to be denied. Private property is now understood to have dual functions. It allows for economic development on one hand, but on the other it has a critical *defensive* function of saving the little man from the excesses of the imperial state. The broad strokes with which Justice Stevens penned his decision showed that he had a tin ear for the populist support for private property institutions. Frozen in the Progressive mindset of his youth, he could not see how uncaring governments and large developers could be regarded as the enemy.

The decision has had odd consequences for a confused public. Judicial activism is still the enemy, and one heartfelt letter in the *Wall Street Journal* denounced *Kelo* as yet another instance of judicial activism, which gets matters 180 degrees backward—the villain of the case is excessive judicial restraint. And the decision has also led to perhaps an overreaction in the opposite direction, given the strong tendency to say that "public use" means, in effect, only two kinds of cases: (1) those where the government takes and operates public facilities or builds and maintains public highways, and (2) those where private owners, such as railroads, operate facilities that are under general common-carrier obligations to take all customers at a reasonable rate.

Justice Stevens had to repudiate that narrow definition, of course, but he did not have to repudiate the entire case law in order to do it. The literal meaning of the phrase "public use" had previously been tested before the Old Court in connection with what has come to be called the holdout problem. Thus, in *Clark v. Nash*,[230] which appears in the same volume of the Supreme Court reporter as *Lochner v. New York,* the Court upheld as "absolutely necessary" the taking of land for an irrigation ditch that was needed to service land that was otherwise arid and valueless.[231] In the next year, 1906, the Court held that an aerial right-of-way over scrubland could be condemned to allow a miner to take his ore from his mine to a nearby railway.[232] Those exceptions go beyond the literal language of public use, but those courts both cautioned that the power was to be used only in exceptional circumstances.

Justice Stevens is correct to note that allowing the condemnation to move forward in these cases requires a broader reading of the term than "use by the public" only. But at the same time he was wholly oblivious to the distinction between baby and giant steps. There is a broad gulf between the requirement that the taking be "absolutely necessary," as the Old Court required, and the modern iteration that allows for "any conceivable" public use.[233] But the rational basis standard invites a determinedly antitheoretical approach to this issue, which is capable of a more rational resolution. The classical liberal position, in opposition to the hard-line libertarian position, has long recognized that cases of "private necessity" should lead to the suspension of ordinary property rights. But it always understood that this exception should never become the thin edge of the wedge that leads to decisions like *Berman, Poletown, Midkiff,* and *Kelo,* all of which are of the Progressive mindset. There is scarcely any better indication that the Old Court, notwithstanding claims about its radical positions, was in fact more nuanced and sensible in its approach than the ham-fisted Progressives who replaced it.

If there is one jurisprudential lesson that should be learned from *Kelo*, it is that the Progressive tradition continues to operate in its bankrupt fashion to the present day. The crushing defeat in *Kelo* is a disaster for the ordinary people who now stand to be thrown unceremoniously out of their homes. But, more than any academic writing could, it may expose the dangerous side of the big-government position that is the hallmark of Progressive thought.

The disposition of these three cases in the 2004 term offers powerful confirmation of the truth that the multiple forces that mold the American constitutional process are mighty and enduring, so that it takes a broad political consensus before any serious shift in constitutional doctrine can be entertained. No single tract can expose the weaknesses of a tradition that has been influential for over 100 years and, on many key issues, dominant for close to 70 years. But, for the record, it should be stated that the Progressive tradition was no more bankrupt on Commerce Clause and economic issues than on matters of race, speech, and religion—bankrupt, moreover, in two distinct but related senses.

The first of these is that it failed as a matter of constitutional interpretation. Although inconsistent on several points, the Framers of the original Constitution, the Bill of Rights, and the Civil War Amendments did start with some strong preference in favor of protecting liberty, property, and the social institutions they foster—competition and free trade in all areas of human endeavor. A good theory of constitutional interpretation is not one that starts and stops with some rote meaning of text, but this charge could not be lodged against the Old Court whose understanding of the need to introduce the nontextual element of the police power shows a sensitivity to structure and function as well as text. Nor can it be said that the interpretation that the justices of the Old Court gave to liberty or property is at variance with ordinary usage or with the larger mission of strong individual protections under a regime of limited government. They made mistakes along the way, and they were forced to make peace with a doctrine that had more protectionist elements than is ideal. But it is hard to charge them with any wholesale betrayal of the original design.

The same cannot be said of the Progressives. They saw in constitutional interpretation the opportunity to rewrite a Constitution that showed at every turn the influence of John Locke and James Madison into a different Constitution, which reflected the wisdom of the leading intellectual reformers of their own time. That effort to switch the terms of discourse fails because it violates the first tenet of interpretation. If you disagree with the original text, then you cannot mend your disagreements by adding to its basic rule some exceptions that change the tenor and purpose of the document. That standard is not meant to privilege the Old Court against modern rivals. The same principle applies to modern constitutions that often are overendowed with positive rights: a right to decent housing does not become a right to purchase decent housing if you can afford it. A grant of positive rights, whether wise or foolish, should not disappear in a blaze of interpretation. The same applies to modern statutes. The National Labor Relations Act should not become the charter of free markets in labor, and the civil rights acts should not be interpreted to allow racial discrimination against any person in the name of ending discrimination. The point here is that anyone on any side of the political spectrum can play fast and loose with authoritative text, and those evasions are no more palatable when done by one side than by the other. The Progressives were wrong on matters of constitutional interpretation because they consciously used their intellectual powers to rewrite, not understand, key provisions of the constitutional text.

Worse perhaps, the Progressives were wrong as a matter of political theory. Assume that they could write their own constitution on a blank slate. What principles of political economy would so captivate their imaginations that they would want to preserve cartels and monopolies in all areas of social life? There are, of course, special cases—patents, telecommunications— where some guarded use of monopoly power may be needed to spur invention or to assemble network industries. But the Progressives were not interested in working through those special cases. Rather, they were determined that their vision of the managed economy should take precedence in all areas of life. Although they purported to have great sophistication on economic and social matters, their understanding of those matters was primitive, and their disdain for the evident signs of social improvement colored their vision of the success of the older order. In the end, they cannot hide behind any notion of judicial restraint or high-minded social virtue. The Progressives and their modern defenders have to live with the stark truth that the noblest innovations of the Progressive Era were its greatest failures.

⟨ Notes ⟩

Preface

1. 198 U.S. 45 (1905).
2. Richard A. Epstein, *Takings: Private Property and the Power of Eminent Domain* (Cambridge, MA: Harvard University Press, 1985).
3. 163 U.S. 537 (1896).
4. 347 U.S. 483 (1954).
5. 334 F.3d 1158, 1160 (D.C. Cir. 2003).

Chapter 1

6. For a detailed and penetrating history of this period, see generally William E. Leuchtenburg, *The Supreme Court Reborn: The Constitutional Revolution in the Age of Roosevelt* (Oxford: Oxford University Press, 1995). Leuchtenburg writes (p. 177), "Within days after [*West Coast Hotel Co. v. Parrish*, 300 U.S. 379 (1937)] was handed down, Washington insiders were regaling one another with a saucy sentence that encapsulated the new legislative situation: 'A switch in time saved nine.'"
7. Justice Owen J. Roberts, who had generally come down against Roosevelt's programs, switched sides in *West Coast Hotel Co.*, which ended the reign of what came to be known as the "Old Court."
8. Roscoe Pound, "Mechanical Jurisprudence," *Columbia Law Review* 8 (1908): 605.
9. Roscoe Pound, "The Need of a Sociological Jurisprudence," *The Green Bag* 19 (1907): 607.
10. Louis D. Brandeis, "The Living Law," *Illinois Law Review* 10 (1917): 461, 463–64.

11. U.S. Bureau of the Census, *Historical Statistics of the United States: Colonial Times to 1957* (Washington, D.C.: Government Printing Office, 1960), p. 72, Series D 36–45.

12. See *infra* at 58–63.

13. U.S. Bureau of the Census, *supra* at note 11 at p. 91, Series D 589–602.

14. Ibid., p. 25, Series B 92–100.

15. Ibid.

16. For a discussion on the health side, see Richard A. Epstein, "In Defense of the 'Old' Public Health: The Legal Framework for the Regulation of Public Health," *Brooklyn Law Review* 69 (2004): 1421.

17. For discussion, see *infra* at notes 18, 29–32, 43–48.

18. 198 U.S. 45, 76 (1905) ("I think that the word 'liberty,' in the 14th Amendment, is perverted when it is held to prevent the natural outcome of a dominant opinion, unless it can be said that a rational and fair man necessarily would admit that the statute proposed would infringe fundamental principles as they have been understood by the traditions of our people and our law.") Note the strong words "perverted" and "necessarily."

19. *Gonzalez v. Raich*, ____U.S.____, 125 Sup. Ct. 2195 (2005), discussed *infra* at 117–20.

20. *Lingle v. Chevron U.S.A., Inc.*, ____U.S.____, 125 Sup. Ct. 2074 (2005), discussed *infra* at 120–24.

21. *Kelo v. City of New London*, ____U.S.____, 125 Sup. Ct. 2655 (2005), discussed *infra* at 124–33.

Chapter 2

22. See, e.g., Richard A. Epstein, *Principles for a Free Society: Reconciling Individual Liberty and the Common Good* (New York: Perseus Books Group, 1998); Richard A. Epstein, *Simple Rules for a Complex World* (Cambridge, MA: Harvard University Press, 1995); Richard A. Epstein, *Skepticism and Freedom: A Modern Case for Classical Liberalism* (Chicago: University of Chicago Press, 2003).

23. For a discussion of the contrasts, see Richard A. Epstein, "Coercion vs. Consent," *Reason*, March 2004, p. 4 (debating Randy Barnett, David Friedman, and James Pinkerton).

24. For further discussion, see Richard A. Epstein, *Free Markets under*

Siege: Cartels, Politics and Social Welfare (Stanford, CA: Hoover Institution Press, 2004).

25. For one recognition thereof in the Progressive Era, see *Barrett v. State*, 116 N.E. 99, 100 (1917).

26. *McCulloch v. Maryland*, 17 U.S. 316, 327 (1819).

27. The traditional accounts included morals and general welfare. See, e.g., *Lochner v. New York*, 198 U.S. 45, 53 (1905) ("Those [police] powers, broadly stated and without, at present, any attempt at a more specific limitation, relate to the safety, health, morals and general welfare of the public. Both property and liberty are held on such reasonable conditions as may be imposed by the governing power of the State in the exercise of those powers, and with such conditions the Fourteenth Amendment was not designed to interfere.").

28. See, e.g., MASS. CONST.; VA. CONST.

29. U.S. CONST. art. I, § 8, cl. 8.

30. Ibid. at art. I, § 8, cl. 4.

31. Ibid. at art. I, § 8, cl. 5.

32. Ibid. at art. I, § 8, cl. 7.

33. Ibid. at art. I, § 8, cls. 15, 16.

34. Ibid. at art. I, § 8, cl. 3.

35. Ibid. at art. I. § 10, cl. 1.

36. Ibid. at art. I. § 10, cl. 2.

37. Alexander Hamilton, "The Federalist No. 11," in *The Federalist Papers*, ed. Clinton Rossiter (New York: Penguin, 1961).

38. Calvin H. Johnson, "The Panda's Thumb: The Modest and Mercantilist Original Meaning of the Commerce Clause," *William and Mary Bill of Rights Journal* 13 (2004): 1. The reference to the panda's thumb is to Stephen Jay Gould, *The Panda's Thumb: More Reflections in Natural History* (New York: W. W. Norton & Company, Inc., 1980), where the thesis was that the panda's so-called thumb was an evolutionary adaptation of a wrist bone into a device for stripping the bamboo shoots, which the panda eats. Johnson's argument is that the Commerce Clause evolved in the direction of free trade.

39. Article I, Section 10, Clause 1 begins "No State shall enter into any Treaty, Alliance, or Confederation. . . ."

40. Article I, Section 2, Clause 2 provides that "No State shall, without the Consent of the Congress, lay any Imposts or Duties on Imports or Exports. . . ." Clause 3 begins in parallel: "No State shall, without the Consent of Congress, lay any Duty of Tonnage . . . ."

41. *The Federalist No. 11, supra* note 37, at p. 90.

42. Donald Regan has argued that "the main point of this grant (unlike the grant of power over foreign commerce) *was not to empower Congress, but rather to disable the states....*" Donald H. Regan, "The Supreme Court and State Protectionism: Making Sense of the Dormant Commerce Clause," *Michigan Law Review* 84 (1986): 1091, 1126 (emphasis added). For a similarly narrow reading of the Commerce Clause, see Randy Barnett, "The Original Meaning of the Commerce Clause," *University of Chicago Law Review* 68 (2001): 101-147; for a contrary account, see Grant S. Nelson & Robert J. Pushaw Jr., "Rethinking the Commerce Clause: Applying First Principles to Uphold Federal Commercial Regulations but Preserve State Control over Social Issues," *Iowa Law Review* 85 (1999): 1–173.

43. 22 U.S. 1 (1824).

44. Ibid. at 190.

45. *Brown v. Maryland,* 25 U.S. 419 (1827).

46. Ibid. at 445.

47. Ibid. at 445–46.

48. *Gibbons,* 22 U.S. at 193–94

49. 27 U.S. 245 (1829).

50. 53 U.S. 299 (1848).

51. Ibid. at 313.

52. 325 U.S. 761 (1945).

53. Compare *South Carolina State Highway Dep't. v. Barnwell Bros.,* 303 U.S. 177 (1938) (sustaining local regulations on length of trucks on narrow mountain roads), with *Kassel v. Consol. Freightways Corp. of Del.,* 450 U.S. 662 (1981) (invalidating a law that prohibited 65-foot double trucks from using Iowa roads). It is possible to think that the *Barnwell* decision gave too much weight to local conditions, however varied, but the entire matter has now been taken out of the constitutional system, for highways now built with federal funds are subject to an administrative procedure to determine whether local safety conditions justify a deviation from the standard rules. See 1982 Surface Transportation Assistance Act, Pub. L. No. 97-424, 96 Stat. 2097.

54. 477 U.S. 131 (1986).

55. Ibid.

56. 156 U.S. 1 (1895).

57. 175 U.S. 211 (1899).

58. 196 U.S. 375 (1905).

59. The point is clear on textual grounds from reading together the Eighteenth Amendment that introduced prohibition in 1919 and the Twenty-first Amendment that repealed it in 1933. The Eighteenth Amendment banned "the manufacture, sale, or transportation of intoxicating liquors, within, the importation thereof into, or the exportation thereof from the United States. . . ." All functions were covered because the Amendment was intended to cover both local and national activities. The Twenty-first Amendment, however, provided that "The transportation or importation into any State, Territory, or possession of the United States for delivery or use therein of intoxicating liquors, in violation of the laws thereof, is hereby prohibited." Note there is no mention of manufacture, which seems odd in an amendment intended to preserve local options over intoxicating spirits. But once it is remembered that manufacture was already within the exclusive control of the states, then there is no need to prohibit the federal regulation thereof, because there is no power to begin with. Only today could one argue that the Congress could require states to allow the manufacture or sale of liquor within state borders even if it were powerless to override state preferences on the transportation or importation of intoxicating spirits.

60. See Harold Demsetz, "Why Regulate Utilities?" *Journal of Law & Economics* 11 (1968): 55; Richard A. Posner, "Natural Monopoly and Its Regulation," *Stanford Law Review* 21 (1969): 548, reprinted in Richard A. Posner, *Natural Monopoly and Its Regulation* (Washington, D.C.: Cato Institute, 1999) (with new foreword by author).

61. 12 East. 530, 104 Eng. Rep. 208 (K.B. 1810).

62. See *Smyth v. Ames*, 169 U.S. 466 (1898).

63. See *Fed. Power Comm'n v. Hope Natural Gas Co.*, 320 U.S. 591 (1944).

64. For the latest Supreme Court effort, see *Duquesne Light Co. v. Barasch*, 488 U.S. 299 (1989).

65. 285 U.S. 262 (1932).

66. Ibid. at 277.

67. Ibid. at 311 (citing Felix Frankfurter, *The Public and Its Government* (Boston, MA: Beacon Press, 1964), pp. 49–51.

68. See Richard A. Epstein, "Exit Rights Under Federalism," *Law and Contemporary Problems* Winter (1992).

69. See, e.g., Adam Smith, *An Inquiry into the Nature and Causes of the Wealth of Nations* (Chicago: University of Chicago Press, reprint 1971), p. 208. ("Monopoly . . . is a great enemy to good management, which

can never be universally established but in consequence of that free and universal competition which forces everybody to have recourse to it for the sake of self-defence.") This passage is instructive because it comes in the context of a discussion of the role that "good roads, canals, and navigable rivers" play in "breaking down the monopoly of the country in its neighbourhood," which touches on the importance of free commerce across state lines, an issue that would not arise in England. Ibid.

70. See *Mitchel v. Reynolds*, 1 P. Wms. 181, 24 Eng. Rep. 347 (Q.B. 1711); for the nineteenth-century version, see *Nordenfelt v. Maxim Nordenfelt Guns & Ammunition Co.*, [1893] 1 Ch. 630.

71. See *supra* at notes 33–36.

72. See *Addyston Pipe & Steel Co. v. United States*, 175 U.S. 211 (1899).

73. *Hammer v. Dagenhart*, 247 U.S. 251 (1918), discussed *infra* at text accompanying notes 99–107. North Carolina had banned labor by children less than 12 years old. Id. at 275.

74. Ernst Freund, *The Police Power: Public Policy and Constitutional Rights* (New York: Callaghan & Company, 1904).

75. Marshall referred to the police power in *Brown v. Maryland*, *supra* note 45, at 443: "The power to direct the removal of gunpowder is a branch of the police power, which unquestionably remains, and ought to remain, with the States."

76. In addition, there is the possibility of protecting unenumerated rights against a broad reading of the police power. "The enumeration in the Constitution of certain rights shall not be construed to deny or disparage others retained by the people." U.S. CONST. Amend. IX. Note that this clause had little role in the pre-1937 period. For a defense of its broad reading, see Randy Barnett, "Reconceiving the Ninth Amendment," *Cornell Law Review* 74 (1988): 1.

77. The first of these defenses allowed the railroad to escape liability to a worker if the worker knowingly assumed an apparent risk incident to his employment. The second held that an individual worker had "impliedly" assumed the risk of any harm caused by his fellow servant during the course of their common employment.

78. 45 U.S.C. § 54 (2005) ("In any action brought against any common carrier under or by virtue of any of the provisions of this chapter to recover damages for injuries to, or the death of, any of its employees, such employee shall not be held to have assumed the risks of his employment in any case where such injury or death resulted in whole or in part from the negligence of any of the officers, agents, or employees of such carrier;

and no employee shall be held to have assumed the risks of his employment in any case where the violation by such common carrier of any statute enacted for the safety of employees contributed to the injury or death of such employee."). For the articulation of the fellow-servant rule, see *Farwell v. Boston & Worcester R.R. Corp.*, 45 Mass. 49, 58–59 (1842). For savage criticism of the rule at the outset of the Progressive period, see 1 Thomas G. Shearman and Amasa A. Redfield, *A Treatise on the Law of Negligence* vi, vii (New York: Baker, Voorhis & Co., 5th ed. 1898).

79. *Second Employer Liability Cases*, 223 U.S. 1, 50 (1912) (quoting *Munn v. Illinois*, 94 U.S. 113, 134 (1876).

80. 243 U.S. 188 (1916).

81. For a discussion, see Richard A. Epstein, "The Historical Origins and Economic Structure of Workers' Compensation," *Georgia Law Review* 16 (1982): 775, 797–808.

82. 198 U.S. 45 (1905).

83. Ibid. at 65.

84. 208 U.S. 161 (1908).

85. 236 U.S. 1 (1915).

86. 245 U.S. 229 (1917), defended in Richard A. Epstein, "A Common Law for Labor Relations: A Critique of the New Deal Labor Legislation," *Yale Law Journal* 92 (1983): 1357. "Yellow-dog contracts" were so named by unions that vilified "yellow dogs" who crossed picket lines.

87. See, e.g., In re Ford Motor Co., 66 N.L.R.B. 1317, 1322 (1946) (excluding from NLRB coverage employees, literally covered under the Act, who advise management in a "confidential capacity"); *NLRB v. Hendricks Cty. Rural Elec. Membership Corp.*, 454 U.S. 170 (1981) (upholding Board exclusion of confidential employees).

Chapter 3

88. 22 U.S. 1 (1824).

89. Ch. 104, 24 Stat. 379 (1887).

90. 234 U.S. 342 (1914).

91. 37 U.S. 72 (1838) (sustaining a statute that imposed penalties against "any person who shall plunder, steal or destroy any money, goods," etc. from a ship under the admiralty jurisdiction of the United States).

92. Ibid. at 78.

Notes

93. See, e.g., *Dairy Stores, Inc. v. Sentinel Publ'g Co.*, 516 A.2d 220 (N.J. 1986) (discussing relationship of defamation to product disparagement).

94. See, e.g., *Evenson v. Spaulding*, 150 F. 517 (9th Cir. 1907).

95. Interstate Commerce Act of 1887, ch. 104, § 4, 24 Stat. 379 (forbidding a railroad "from charging or receiving" more for a short-haul run than for the long-haul run of which it was a part).

96. 234 U.S. at 351–52 (citations omitted).

97. Transportation Act of 1920, ch. 91, 41 Stat. 456.

98. 257 U.S. 563 (1922).

99. 247 U.S. 251 (1918).

100. Ibid. at 277.

101. Charles Tiebout, "A Pure Theory of Local Expenditures," *Journal of Political Economy* 64 (1956): 416.

102. For a discussion, see Richard A. Epstein, "Exit Rights and Insurance Regulation: From Federalism to Takings," *George Mason Law Review* 7 (1999): 293.

103. 347 U.S. 483 (1954).

104. 247 U.S. at 273.

105. Felix Frankfurter, "Child Labor and the Court," *The New Republic*, July 26, 1922, 248.

106. *Bailey v. Drexel Furniture Co.*, 259 U.S. 20 (1922).

107. Frankfurter, *supra* note 105 at 248–49.

108. Here is one account of the consequences of the tariff issued by the U.S. Department of State:

> The Smoot-Hawley Tariff was more a consequence of the onset of the Great Depression than an initial cause. But while the tariff might not have caused the Depression, it certainly did not make it any better. It provoked a storm of foreign retaliatory measures and came to stand as a symbol of the 'beggar-thy-neighbor' policies (policies designed to improve one's own lot at the expense of that of others) of the 1930s. Such policies contributed to a drastic decline in international trade. For example, U.S. imports from Europe declined from a 1929 high of $1,334 million to just $390 million in 1932, while U.S. exports to Europe fell from $2,341 million in 1929 to $784 million in 1932. Overall, world trade declined by some 66 percent between 1929 and 1934. More generally, Smoot-Hawley did nothing to foster trust and cooperation among nations in either the political or the economic realm during a perilous era in international relations.

U.S. Department of State, Smoot-Hawley Tariff, *at* http://www.state.gov/r/pa/ho/time/id/17606.htm (visited March 18, 2005).

109. 15 U.S.C. § 703.

110. 295 U.S. 495 (1935).

111. Ibid. at 542–43.

112. 301 U.S. 1 (1937). Note that the government's name appears first in the case because it had in fact lost on Commerce Clause grounds in the three lower court decisions that had considered the case.

113. *Wickard v. Filburn,* 317 U.S. 111, 126 (1942).

114. 315 U.S. 110 (1942).

115. 317 U.S. 111 (1942).

116. See, e.g., Thurman Arnold, *The Folklore of Capitalism* (Westport, CT: Greenwood Press, 1937).

117. 317 U.S. at 120.

118. *Gibbons v. Ogden,* 22 U.S. 1, 197 (1824).

119. *Wrightwood,* 315 U.S. at 119.

120. *Gibbons,* 22 U.S. at 194 (emphasis added).

121. U.S. CONST. art. I, § 8, cl. 18.

122. *Wickard,* 317 U.S. at 119, 121.

123. 188 U.S. 321 (1903).

124. 17 U.S. 316 (1819).

125. *Gibbons,* 22 U.S. at 187–88.

126. 514 U.S. 549 (1995).

127. 529 U.S. 598 (2000).

128. 18 U.S.C. § 922(q)(1)(A) (1995).

129. *Addyston Pipe & Steel Co. v. United States*, 175 U.S. 211 (1899).

130. *Hartford Fire Insurance Co. v. California,* 509 U.S. 764 (1993).

131. 15 U.S.C. §§ 61–66 (1994), discussed in A. Paul Victor, "Export Cartels: An Idea Whose Time Has Passed," *Antitrust Law Journal* 60 (1991): 571. One could add, "Or Never Came."

132. 291 U.S. 502 (1934).

133. Ibid. at 538 (footnotes omitted).

134. Ibid. at 518 n.2 (citing Laws of 1933, ch. 158, art. 25).

135. On McReynolds's mixed legacy, see James E. Bond, *I Dissent: The Legacy of Chief Justice James Clark McReynolds* (Fairfax, VA: George Mason University Press, 1992).

136. 291 U.S. at 557–58.

137. See *Baldwin v. G.A.F. Seelig,* 294 U.S. 511 (1935), decided one year after *Nebbia.*

Notes

138. 483 U.S. 266 (1987).

139. See *Armco, Inc. v. Hardesty*, 467 U.S. 638, 644 (1984).

140. 317 U.S. 341 (1943).

141. 15 U.S.C. § 17 (2000).

142. For a modern discussion of the tension, see, e.g., *Duquesne Light Co. v. Barasch*, 488 U.S. 299, 307–16 (1989).

143. Richard B. Freeman & James L. Medoff, *What Unions Do* (New York: Basic Books, 1984).

144. See *supra* at note 85.

145. 254 U.S. 443 (1921).

146. Ibid. at 468–72 (stating that courts may not enjoin the normal operations of labor unions under the Clayton Act).

147. Ibid. at 479–80.

148. 208 U.S. 161 (1908).

149. 236 U.S. 1 (1915).

150. 245 U.S. 229 (1917).

151. 208 U.S. 412 (1908).

152. Brief for Appellant, 1908 U.S. LEXIS 1452, at ***2.

153. 208 U.S. at 422–23.

154. 83 U.S. 130 (1873).

155. Sylvia A. Law, "Rethinking Sex and the Constitution," *University of Pennsylvania Law Review* 132 (1984): 1005.

156. 300 U.S. 379 (1937).

157. Ibid. at 398–99.

158. Ibid. at 400.

159. Felix Frankfurter, "Law and Order," *Yale Review* 10 (1920): 233–34.

160. Pub. L. No. 74-198, 49 Stat. 449 (codified as amended at 29 U.S.C. §§ 151–169).

161. 29 U.S.C. § 151.

162. See *supra* at notes 5–7.

163. See *Loewe v. Lawlor*, 208 U.S. 274 (1908).

164. 250 U.S. 616 (1919). The case marked a welcome reversal from Holmes's earlier decision upholding a similar conviction in *Schenck v. United States*, 249 U.S. 47 (1919).

165. 249 U.S. at 52.

166. See Geoffrey R. Stone, *Perilous Times* (New York: W.W. Norton & Company, 2004), pp. 135–233.

167. 250 U.S. at 630.

168. 163 U.S. 537 (1896), overruled by *Brown v. Bd. of Educ.*, 347 U.S. 483 (1954).

169. Lawrence J. Friedman, *The White Savage Racial Fantasies in the Postbellum South* (Upper Saddle River, N.J.: Prentice Hall, 1970), p. 160.

170. Charles Paul Freund, "Dixiecrats Triumphant: The Menacing Mr. Wilson," *Reason Online,* Dec. 18, 2002, http://reason.com/links/links 121802.shmtl (visited Jan. 14, 2005) (citing Friedman, *supra* at note 169, at 150–68 (1970)).

171. 262 U.S. 390 (1923).

172. 268 U.S. 510 (1925).

173. 262 U.S. at 397–98.

174. Ibid. at 399.

175. 268 U.S. at 534–35 (citation omitted).

176. *Bartels v. Iowa,* 262 U.S. 404, 412 (1923) (Holmes, J., dissenting).

177. Ibid.

178. "Can the Supreme Court Guarantee Toleration?" *The New Republic,* June 17, 1925, at 85, 86. The editorial appears in Felix Frankfurter, *Felix Frankfurter on the Supreme Court,* ed. Philip B. Kurland (Cambridge, MA: Belknap Press, 1970), p. 174.

179. Frankfurter, *supra* at note 178.

180. 274 U.S. 200, 207 (1927).

181. Ibid.

182. For the tragic story, see William E. Leuchtenburg, "Mr. Justice Holmes and Three Generations of Imbeciles," in *The Supreme Court Reborn: The Constitutional Revolution in the Age of Roosevelt* (Oxford: Oxford University Press, 1995), p. 3. Leuchtenburg writes: "The Supreme Court has never found occasion to reverse *Buck v. Bell,* and as late as 1980, compulsory sterilization laws were still on the books in more than twenty states, including Virginia," the state whose statute was upheld in *Buck.* Id. at p. 24. A 1981 Virginia law "sharply circumscribed" the circumstances under which sterilizations could be performed but still permits them. Id. at p. 25. The relevant state statutes appear to permit them only for individuals incapable of consent. Va. Code Ann. § 54.1-2975; Va. Code. Ann. § 54.1-2976. The only dissenter in *Buck* was the conservative Pierce Butler, who might have been more motivated by his Catholic faith than a broad view of individual liberties. Leuchtenburg, *supra* at 14–15.

183. 310 U.S. 586 (1940), overruled by *W. Va. Bd. of Educ. v. Barnette,* 319 U.S. 624 (1943).

Notes

184. Ibid. at 596.

185. 319 U.S. 624 (1943).

186. Ibid. at 642.

187. Ibid. at 646 (Frankfurter, J., dissenting).

188. Ibid. at 647 (Frankfurter, J., dissenting).

Chapter 4

189. 304 U.S. 144 (1938).

190. Ibid. at 153 n.4.

191. See, e.g., *Loretto v. Teleprompter Manhattan CATV Corp.*, 458 U.S. 419 (1982).

192. See *Penn Cent. Transp. Co. v. City of New York*, 438 U.S. 104 (1978), where Justice Brennan despairs of finding anything other than "ad hoc" rules to decide takings cases.

193. 304 U.S. at 153 n.4.

194. Ibid. (some citations omitted).

Chapter 5

195. 514 U.S. 549 (1995).

196. ____U.S. ____, 125 Sup. Ct. 2195 (2005), rev'g 352 F.3d 1222 (9th Cir. 2003). I worked with the Institute for Justice in preparing an amicus brief in support of plaintiff-appellant Angel Raich.

197. Cal. Health & Safety Code § 11362.5 (2005).

198. Controlled Substances Act (CSA), 21 U.S.C. §§ 801 et seq. (2005).

199. In an earlier decision, the Supreme Court had held that Congress had intended to trump all state laws when it passed the CSA but left the Commerce Clause issue unresolved. See *United States v. Oakland Cannabis Buyers' Cooperative*, 532 U.S. 483, 494 n.7 (2001).

200. 317 U.S. 111 (1942).

201. See, e.g., findings 3 and 4 of the CSA, which read:

(3) A major portion of the traffic in controlled substances flows through interstate and foreign commerce. Incidents of the traffic which are not an integral part of the interstate or foreign flow, such as manufacture, local distribution, and possession, nonetheless have a substantial and direct effect upon interstate commerce because—

(A) after manufacture, many controlled substances are transported in interstate commerce,

(B) controlled substances distributed locally usually have been transported in interstate commerce immediately before their distribution, and

(C) controlled substances possessed commonly flow through interstate commerce immediately prior to such possession.

(4) Local distribution and possession of controlled substances contribute to swelling the interstate traffic in such substances.

21 U.S.C. § 801(3)–(4) (2005).

202. *People ex rel. Lungren v. Peron*, 70 Cal. Rptr. 2d 20, 23 (1997) (recounting abuses), cited in *Raich*, 125 Sup. Ct. at 2215 n.43 by Justice Stevens.

203. 125 Sup. Ct. at 2229–39 (Thomas, J., dissenting).

204. Ibid. at 2212 n.37 ("We acknowledge that evidence proffered by respondents in this case regarding the effective medical uses for marijuana, if found credible after trial, would cast serious doubt on the accuracy of the findings that require marijuana to be listed in Schedule I. See, e.g., Institute of Medicine, *Marijuana and Medicine: Assessing the Science Base*, ed. J. Joy, S. Watson, & J. Benson (Washington, D.C.: National Academy Press, 1999), p. 179: (recognizing that "[s]cientific data indicate the potential therapeutic value of cannabinoid drugs, primarily THC [Tetrahydrocannabinol] for pain relief, control of nausea and vomiting, and appetite stimulation").

205. See, supra at notes 38–41.

206. The list includes Alaska, Arizona, Colorado, Hawaii, Maine, Nevada, Oregon, Vermont, and Washington. See *Raich*, 125 Sup. Ct. at 2198 n.1.

207. On this score the resignation of Justice O'Connor, which was followed by the death of Chief Justice Rehnquist, would not change matters since both dissented in *Raich*.

208. _____ U.S. _____, 125 Sup. Ct. 2074 (2005), rev'g 363 F.3d 846 (9th Cir. 2004). Mark Moller of the Cato Institute and I authored a brief in *Lingle*, urging the Court to affirm the decision below on the merits. Brief of Amicus Curiae the Cato Institute, *Lingle* (No. 04-163), available at http://www.cato.org/pubs/legalbriefs/epstein_brief.pdf (last visited July 17, 2005).

209. Hawaii Act 257, Haw. Rev. Stat. § 486H-10.4 (1997).

210. 447 U.S. 255 (1980).

Notes

211. Ibid. at 260.

212. *Lingle*, 125 Sup. Ct. at 2077.

213. 438 U.S. 104 (1978).

214. 125 Sup. Ct. at 2081–82 (citations omitted). It is worth noting that *Lingle* did more than impose a rent control statute. Its territorial restrictions on new entry are a classic form of protectionism that normally is attacked as a limitation on economic liberties.

215. For my more extensive critique of this decision, and those that follow in its wake, see Richard A. Epstein, "The Ebbs and Flows in Takings Law: Reflections on the *Lake Tahoe* Case," in *Cato Supreme Court Review* 5, ed. Mark Moller (Washington, D.C.: The Cato Institute, 2002).

216. 125 Sup. Ct. at 2082 (citing *Penn Cent. Transp. Co.*, 438 U.S. at 124).

217. ____ U.S. ____, 125 Sup. Ct. 2655 (2005). Once again on behalf of the Cato Institute, Mark Moller and I authored a brief in support of Kelo in the Supreme Court. I am also proud to acknowledge my close working relationship with the Institute for Justice, which worked so hard on behalf of Kelo and her fellow owners, and which continues to work on the case even after the Supreme Court has spoken.

218. U.S. CONST. amend V.

219. See, for one account, Timothy Egan, Ruling Sets Off Tug of War Over Private Property, N.Y. Times, July 29, 2005, at A1.

220. 348 U.S. 26 (1954).

221. Ibid. at 33 (citation omitted).

222. 304 N.W.2d 455 (Mich. 1981).

223. 684 N.W.2d 765 (Mich. 2004).

224. 467 U.S. 229 (1984).

225. Ibid. at 241, quoted in *Kelo*, 125 Sup. Ct. at 2669 (Kennedy, J., concurring).

226. 125 Sup. Ct. at 2669 (Kennedy, J., concurring).

227. 467 U.S. at 233–34.

228. 125 Sup. Ct. at 2661.

229. 467 U.S. at 241–42.

230. See 125 Sup. Ct. at 2676–77 (O'Connor, J., dissenting).

231. 198 U.S. 361 (1905).

232. Ibid. at 370.

233. *Strickley v. Highland Boy Gold Mining Co.*, 200 U.S. 527 (1906).

234. See 125 Sup. Ct. at 2662–63.

☙ Index ❧

Index

About the Author

Richard A. Epstein is the James Parker Hall Distinguished Service Professor of Law at the University of Chicago and the Peter and Kirsten Senior Fellow at the Hoover Institution. He is a former editor of the *Journal of Legal Studies* and of the *Journal of Law and Economics*. His books include *Skepticism and Freedom: A Modern Case for Classical Liberalism* (2003), *Principles for a Free Society: Reconciling Individual Liberty with the Common Good* (1998), *Simple Rules for a Complex World* (1995), *Forbidden Grounds: The Case Against Employment Discrimination Laws* (1992), and *Takings: Private Property and the Power of Eminent Domain* (1985). He is an adjunct scholar of the Cato Institute.

Cato Institute

Founded in 1977, the Cato Institute is a public policy research foundation dedicated to broadening the parameters of policy debate to allow consideration of more options that are consistent with the traditional American principles of limited government, individual liberty, and peace. To that end, the Institute strives to achieve greater involvement of the intelligent, concerned lay public in questions of policy and the proper role of government.

The Institute is named for *Cato's Letters*, libertarian pamphlets that were widely read in the American Colonies in the early 18th century and played a major role in laying the philosophical foundation for the American Revolution.

Despite the achievement of the nation's Founders, today virtually no aspect of life is free from government encroachment. A pervasive intolerance for individual rights is shown by government's arbitrary intrusions into private economic transactions and its disregard for civil liberties.

To counter that trend, the Cato Institute undertakes an extensive publications program that addresses the complete spectrum of policy issues. Books, monographs, and shorter studies are commissioned to examine the federal budget, Social Security, regulation, military spending, international trade, and myriad other issues. Major policy conferences are held throughout the year, from which papers are published thrice yearly in the *Cato Journal*. The Institute also publishes the quarterly magazine *Regulation*.

In order to maintain its independence, the Cato Institute accepts no government funding. Contributions are received from foundations, corporations, and individuals, and other revenue is generated from the sale of publications. The Institute is a nonprofit, tax-exempt, educational foundation under Section 501(c)3 of the Internal Revenue Code.

CATO INSTITUTE
1000 Massachusetts Ave., N.W.
Washington, D.C. 20001
www.cato.org